Ringerike Style Essentials

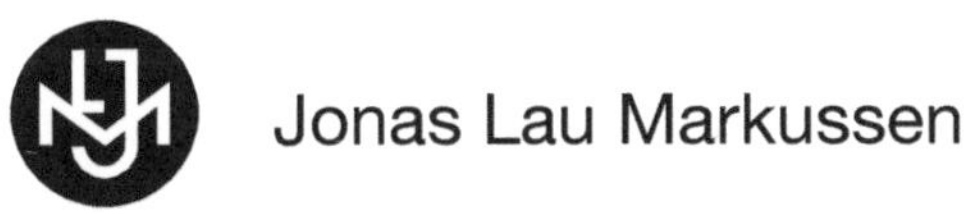

Jonas Lau Markussen

Ringerike Style Essentials — How to Create Viking Age Art
Jonas Lau Markussen

1st edition
ISBN 978-87-970600-8-7

Contents

Introduction

The Ringerike Style

The Ringerike style (c. 1000-1075 CE) is one of the quintessential styles of the Viking Age. Its abundant and elegant knotwork patterns are demonstrably appealing to a modern audience, not least for many seeking to adorn their body with a lasting piece of artwork rooted in historical Nordic customs.

But how do you recreate the style in accordance with its original principles? For a contemporary audience, the concepts of the intricate interlacing patterns can seem incomprehensible and daunting to understand and replicate.

This book unlocks the secrets of the enigmatic craft of knotwork creation and makes it approachable for you to create your own designs.

The Building Blocks

The book is organised into two main sections. The first part will introduce you to all the necessary building blocks needed to create your Ringerike-style design.

The style employs a very particular selection of simple visual elements and concepts like, for example, acanthus leaves and pretzel knots to compose the intricate knotwork compositions.

This handful of simple compositional elements is combined, repeated and reconfigured over and over throughout a composition. If you know these, you can virtually create any Ringerike-style composition imaginably.

At the beginning of each chapter, you'll find suggestions for easy exercises that'll help you familiarise yourself with the concepts presented and make them stick.

The Design Process

The second section will walk you through the process of creating your Ringerike-style design step-by-step. You'll combine all the building blocks into a fully-fledged *great beast* composition.

The iconic great beast motif comprises a lion or wolf-like creature opposing a serpent or vine wrapped around its body. The motif is known originally from the greater Jelling stone. It is a stable design throughout the late Viking Age, featured on numerous runestones throughout Scandinavia and the surrounding Norse-influenced regions.

You'll learn how to construct an intricate knotwork-based composition. From analysing the references to laying out the composition's main lines and shaping the ornament's details.

Tools and Setup

A basic understanding of illustration is preferable. You'll definitely be off to a much easier start if you know how to operate a pen, as I won't go into the basics of illustration.

This book's principles and concepts apply to virtually all visual media and crafts. You can replicate the process digitally or traditionally with pen and paper. If you have a personal preference and a medium you are comfortable with, stick to that.

Before you begin, I'd recommend you check out *The Anatomy of Viking Art*. It is a great companion guide and a quick introduction to the core concepts and periods of Viking Age art, including the Ringerike style.

I hope you'll enjoy your time getting into the Ringerike style in the company of this book and that it will serve you as an excellent compendium for revisiting and referencing long after you've created your first design.

Let's get started!

The Building Blocks

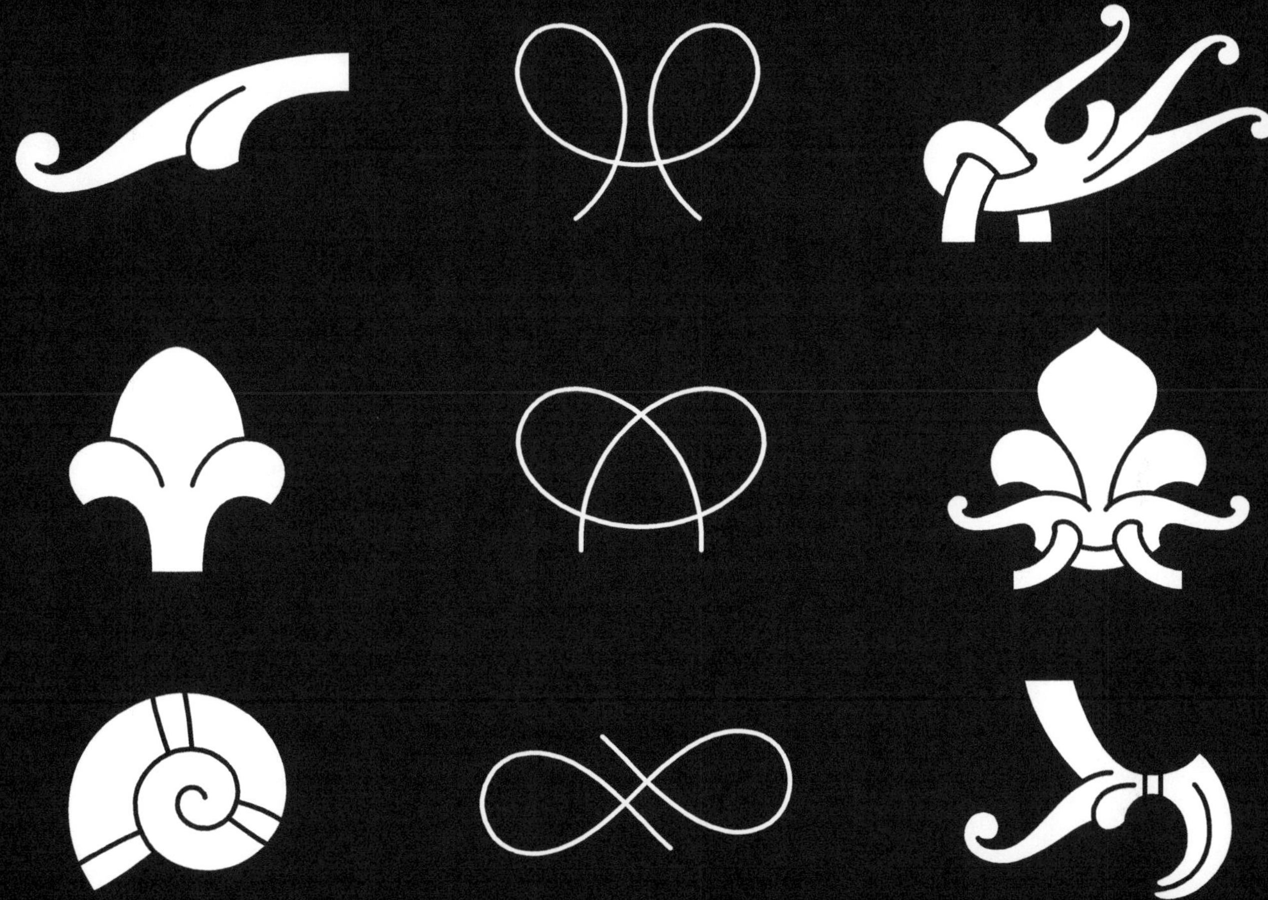

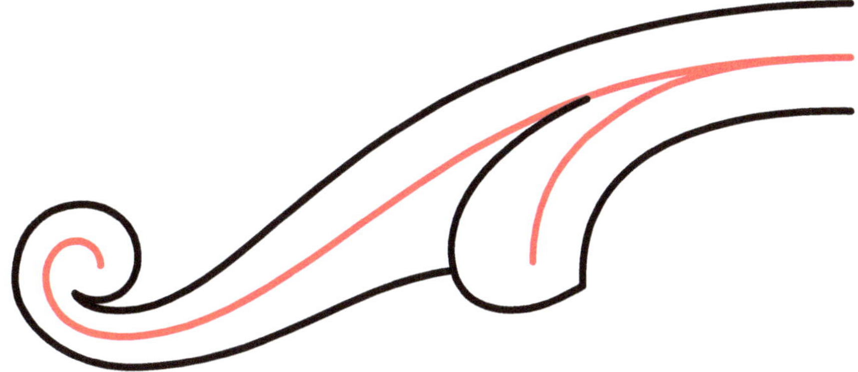

Ribbons and Motifs

Ribbons and ornamental motifs are the two most essential types of building blocks in a Ringerike-style design.

All compositions are built on the principles of interlacing patterns of ribbons, even the most simple ones.

These simple yet, intricate knotwork designs are dressed in numerous variations of the same vegetal motifs, like leaves and spirals created from a few core template shapes.

Even animal limbs and features are created from these vegetal building blocks, and their limbs and bodies act as ribbons in the interlace pattern, sprouting additional ribbon strands.

Exercises

Take a look at the Ringerike-style designs at the back of the book. Can you identify each of the motifs and features described in the chapter?

Try recreating the motifs and features. Start with sketching the simple ornamental motifs one by one, and move on to the animals. Keep it quick and rough; it's all about getting familiar with the style rather than making a perfect masterpiece.

Ribbons

Terminals

Knotwork ribbons are generally even-width, and at least one of the ribbon's ends is virtually always terminated by a tight spiral ball.

The other end might be shaped like an animal head if the ribbon constitutes an animal, like a serpent.

If it's vegetal, the ribbon may be shooting off from a base, like a branch off a trunk. The spiral ball terminal is usually accompanied by a side lobe, creating an acanthus leaf.

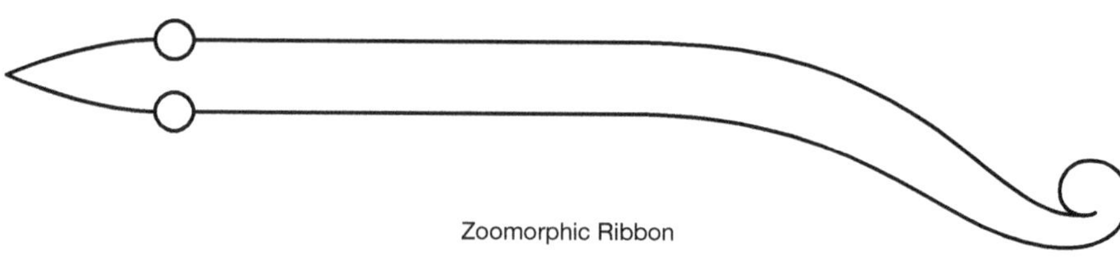
Zoomorphic Ribbon

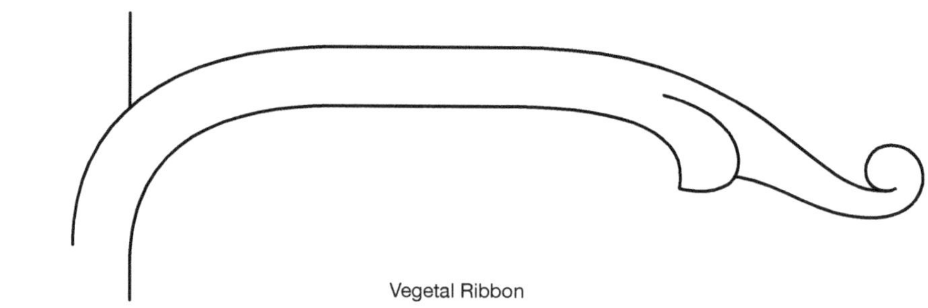
Vegetal Ribbon

Widths

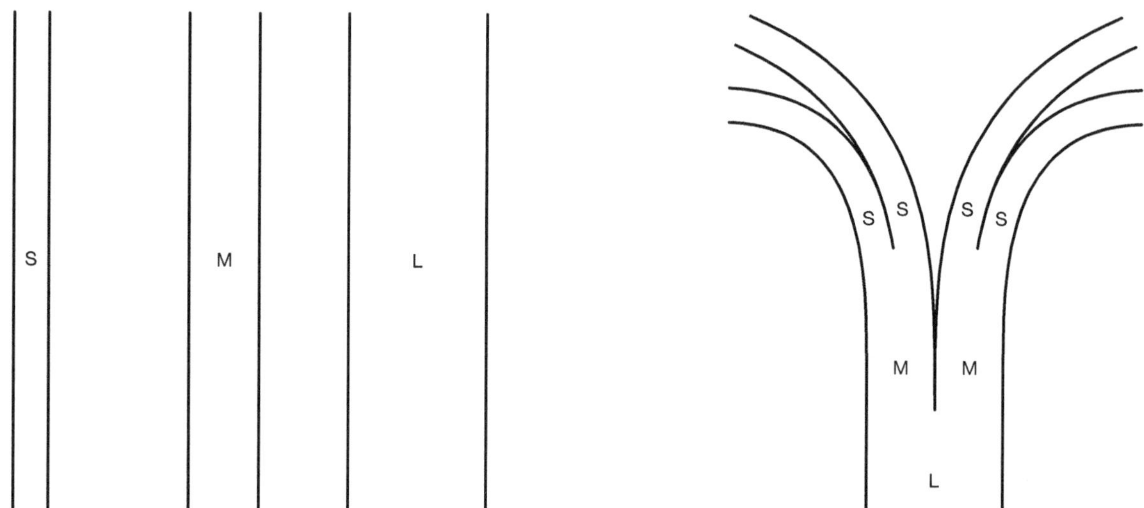

Tiers

Knotwork patterns often consist of a select range of ribbon widths. The ribbons of a design can usually be divided into two or more consistent tiers, keeping to a set width within their respective tier level. Their width roughly correlates with their structural role in the composition.

Structure

It's helpful to think of these levels as, for example, a three-tiered tree structure consisting of a wide stem or trunk rooted at the base (L), with thinner branches shooting off from it further up (M) before splitting into slim twigs carrying the foliage at the ends (S).

Strands

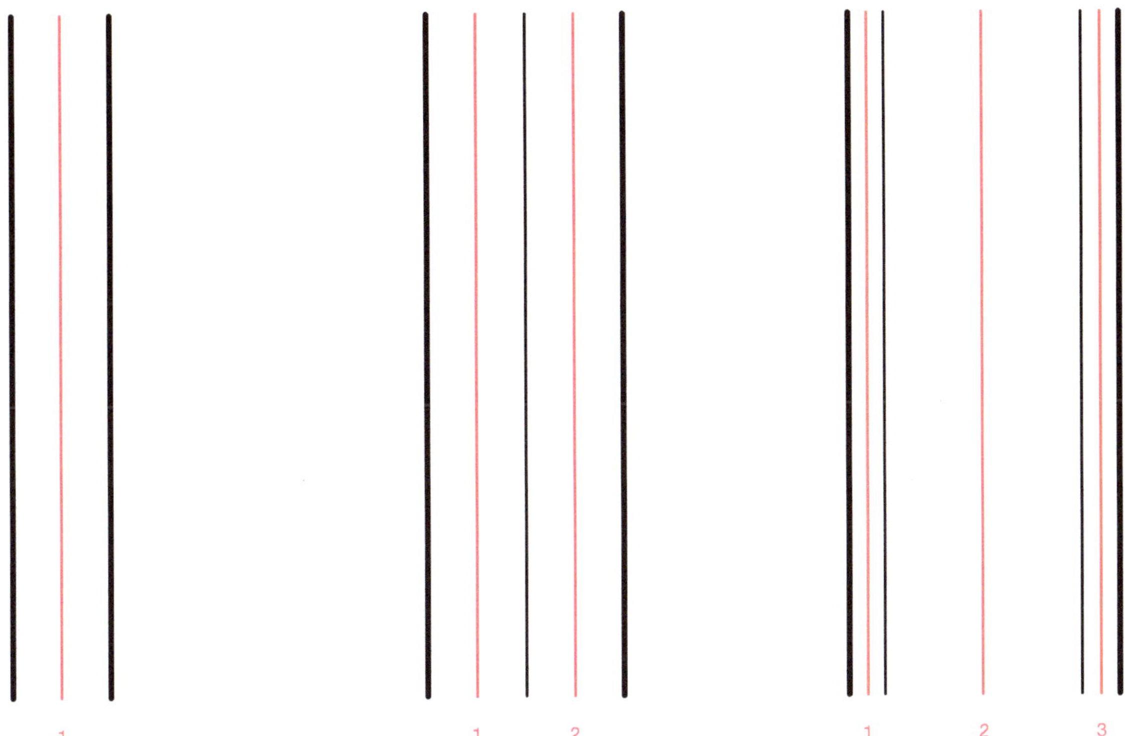

Regular

A regular single-stranded ribbon is the core element of all the interlacing patterns.

Double

Ribbons are often split into two or more parallel equal-width strands. Multi-stranded ribbons create more opportunities for elaborate details. For example by:

- Adding more ribbon elements to the interlacing pattern, creating a denser weave.
- Acting as a mechanism for creating offshoots by forking a ribbon in two.
- Or by joining two ribbons into one, as is often the case with the contour lines of larger animals coming together to create a double-stranded tail.

Double-strands are most common, but triple- or more multi-strands occur.

Contoured

Multi-stranded ribbons also come in multi-width configurations. Wide ribbons may have slim strands lining the edge like a contour. This is especially common with the bodies of larger animals.

Interlace

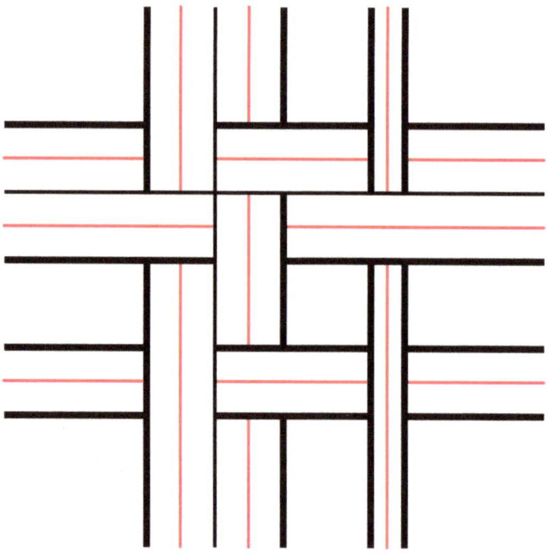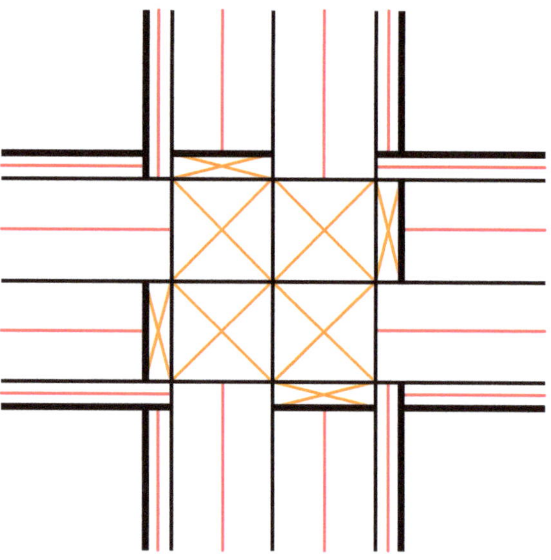

Loose weave

Ribbons are generally woven and looped loosely with a bit of room in-between each other to create an easy flow of the ribbons for an evenly distributed knotwork pattern.

In a loose weave, it's always clear where the visible ribbon elements are going and how they are flowing and weaving into each other.

Tight weave

Sometimes, bits of tightly woven ribbons occur and create an interesting contrast to the rest of the loosely woven ornament.

Multi-stranded ribbons woven tightly together create a segmentation effect, almost exploding the interlacing ribbons into an abstract tile-like pattern.

In a tight weave, the visible ribbon elements lose their context. The direction of each ribbon is lost in the tile pattern of the segmented ribbons.

Snippets

Ribbon segmentation also plays a role in another ornamental element, the ribbon snippet.

Ribbon snippets are short rectangular pieces of ribbon inserted perpendicular across another ribbon; their length equals the width of the ribbon it's going across.

They look like they are wrapped tightly around the ribbon they're crossing.

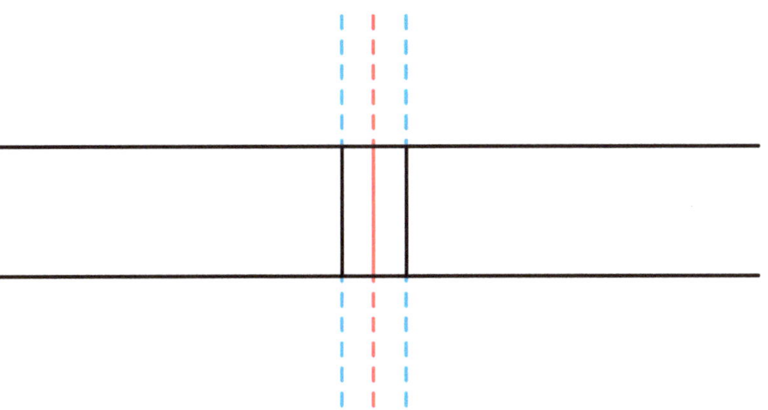

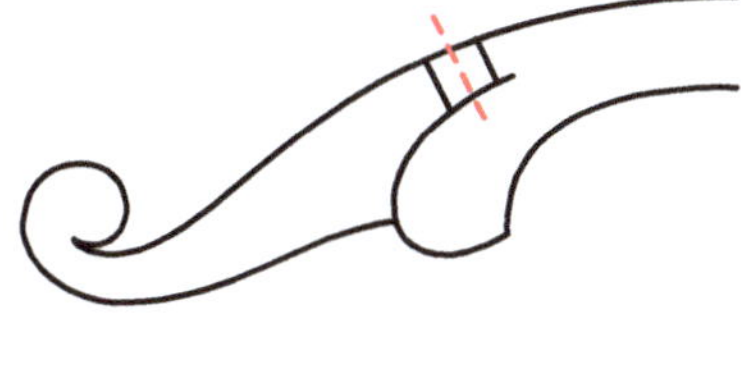

A

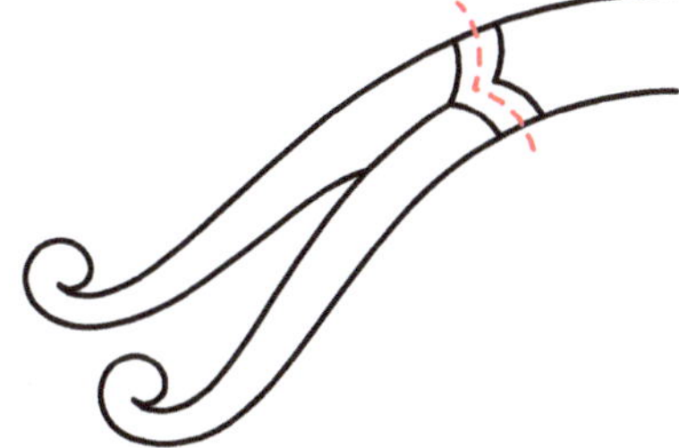

B

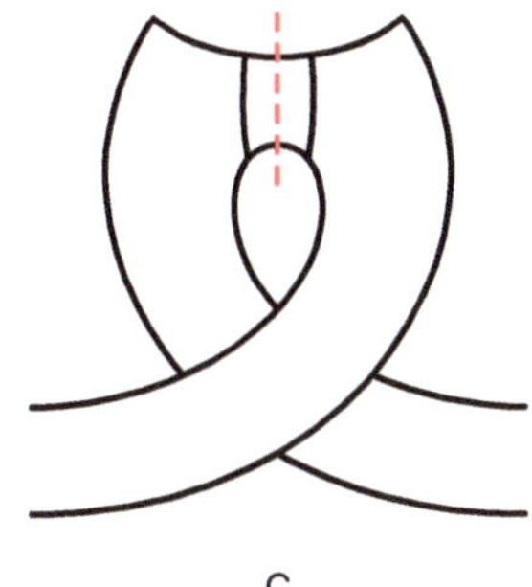

C

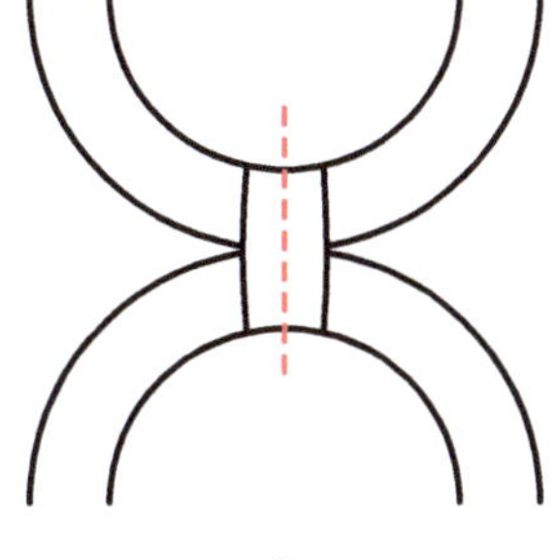

D

In application

Snippets are generally applied to convey a connection between elements, like an ornamental linchpin inserted in between two ribbon elements. Either as a transition of one element shooting off another (A) or a strand splitting into multiple lesser strands (B).

Or as a binding element enforcing the tip of a loop's curve by tightening the ribbon creating a concave dent (C), or holding two contour ribbons tightly together in a tie (D).

Ribbon snippets occur in the shape of a simple rectangular pellet-shaped chip (A, C, D) or a curvy V-shape (B) reminiscent of the centre part of a union-knot ribbon where it splits in two.

Ornamental Motifs

A characteristic trait of the Ringerike style is its repetitive use of particular visual elements.

Ornamental tropes are extensively duplicated and juxtaposed repeatedly to create a cornucopian effect of abundance.

The shape and silhouette of each ornamental motif is constructed by the underlying flow of one or more ribbon strands or ends.

Acanthus Leaf

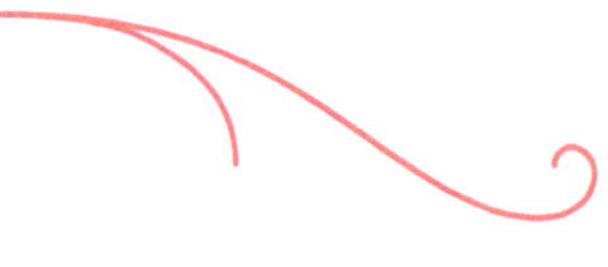

Palmette

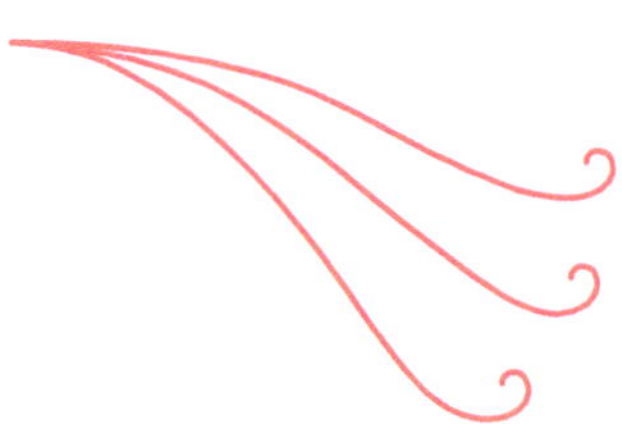

Ribbons

The acanthus leaf's main ribbon flows in a slight S-curve, curling up into a tight spiral at the end. A short offshoot is forking out and curling down and slightly backwards.

The palmette's stem ribbon forks out into two or more S-shaped prongs, each curling up into tight spirals at the end.

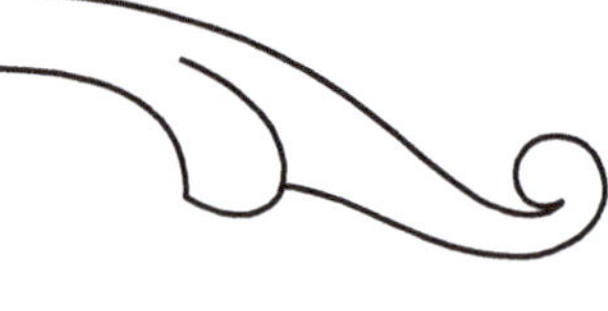

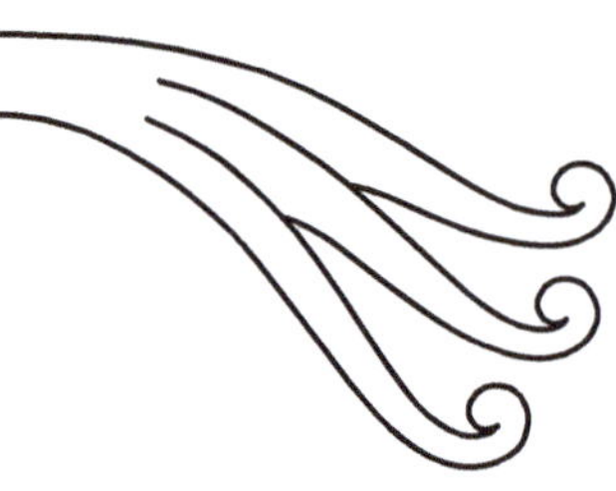

Shape

The shape of the acanthus leaf is very slender and slightly tapered, the tip curling tightly into a ball shape. The side lobe is fanning out like a slightly curled teardrop-shape widest at the bottom. The leaf is usually the widest, where the bottom outline attaches to the front of the side lobe.

The palmette's ribbon prongs are slender and almost even. The spirals usually curl tightly into a ball shape similar to the tip of the acanthus leaf.

Fleur-de-lis

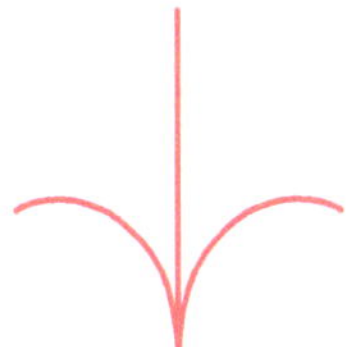

The fleur-de-lis's stem ribbon forks out into three strands. A straight centre prong, with an outwards curling prong at each side, mirroring each other.

Union Knot

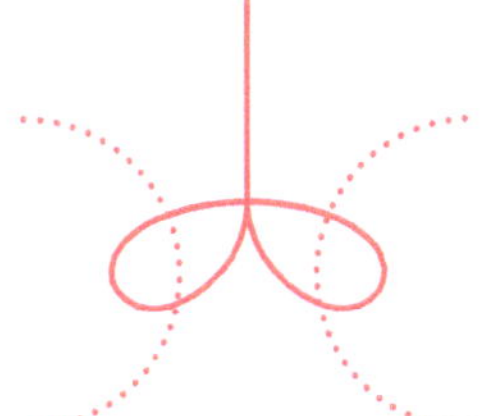

The union knot's ribbon begins as a straight line splitting into two strands towards the bottom, each curling in opposite directions before joining again at the centre, crossing the main ribbon. The loops of the two strands curl around adjacent ribbons of the ornament.

Spiral

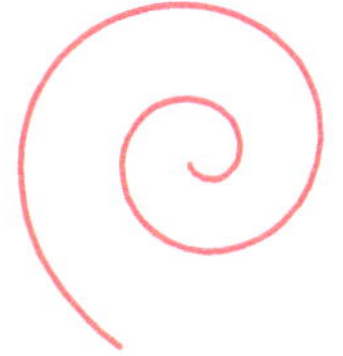

The spiral's ribbon usually curls around a couple of times on itself.

Dented Loop

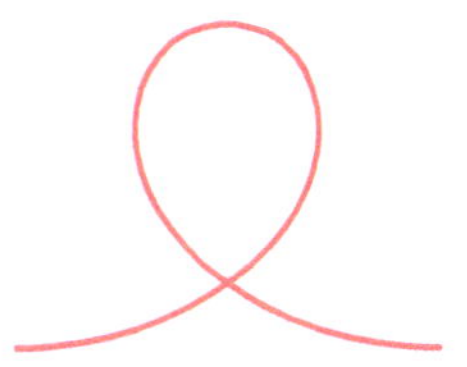

The dented loop's ribbon curls in an even pear-shaped single loop.

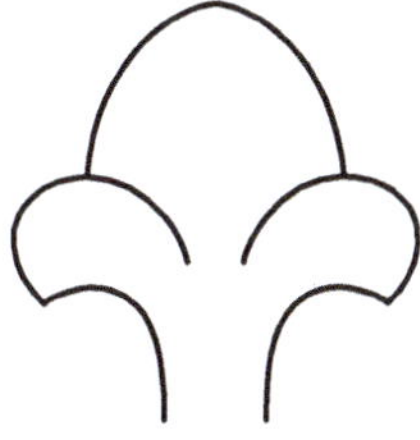

The fleur-de-lis's centre leaf is usually tongue-shaped, sometimes leaning towards diamond-shaped. The side lobes are shaped like the acanthus leaf's side lobe and behave similarly.

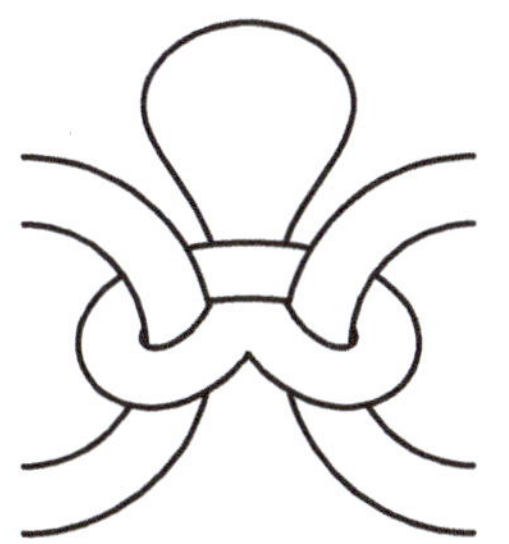

The union knot's main ribbon is tongue-shaped before it tapers in and splits in two. The two strands of the adjacent ribbon loops are even and of equal width.

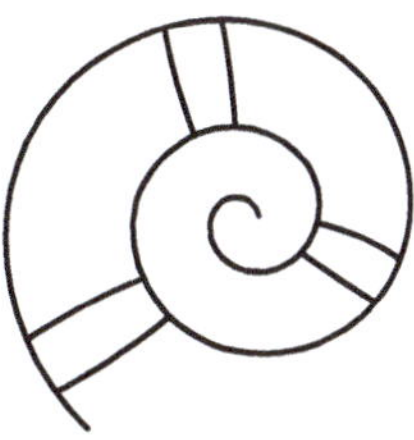

The spiral's ribbon is slightly narrower at the centre and broader at the edge where it opens up. The spiralling ribbon is often segmented into three or more parts by ribbon snippets intersecting the curling strand perpendicularly.

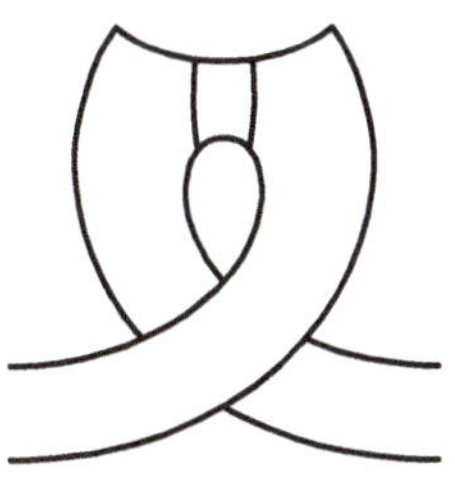

The dented loop's ribbon is of equal width at the beginning and end but widens at the top of the loop. The top of the loop is pressed down towards the centre, creating a concave dent with sharp corners at each side of the indentation. The compressed part of the indented loop is often split by a ribbon snippet crossing the loop's top perpendicularly.

Serpents

Head

Minimal
A serpent's head is usually seen in bids-eye-view. The overall shape is triangular, tapering in from the neck to the tip of the nose. The two round eyes sit in the centre of the outline at each side of the head, where the tapering begins.

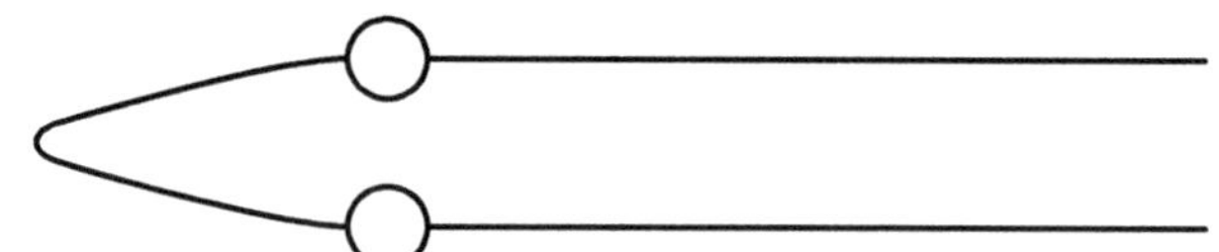

Simple
A ribbon snippet connecting the eyes is a common element, sometimes accompanied by a line running down the centre of the head. Tongues occur on several runestones, either as a single line or as a crow's feet-like shape of three lines protruding from the tip.

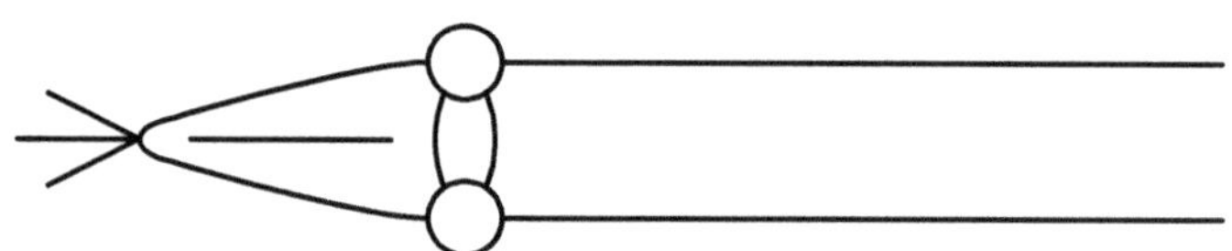

Classic
The centre line sometimes runs all the way into the tip, splitting the head and articulating the two jaws seen in profile. Lobe-shaped eyebrows curling halfway around the eyes occur in more elaborate examples.

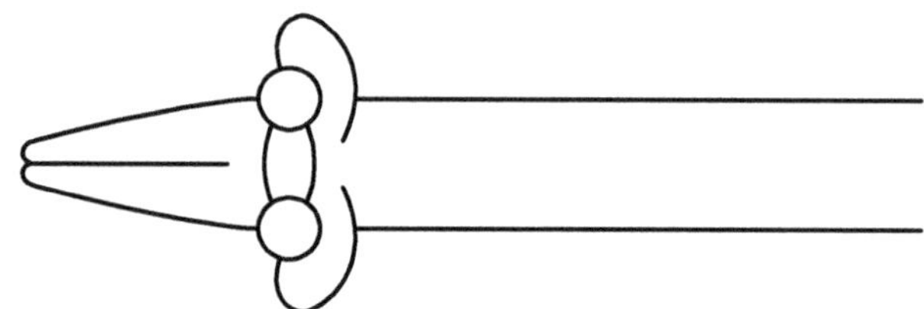

Alternate
Boat-shaped eyes occur in some late Ringerike-style examples trending towards the Urnes style.

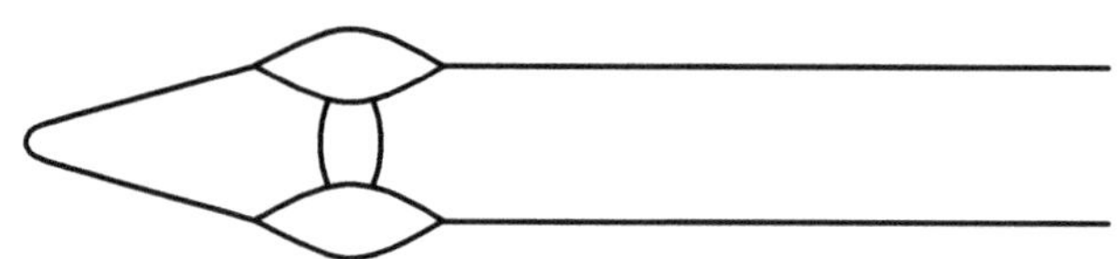

Tail

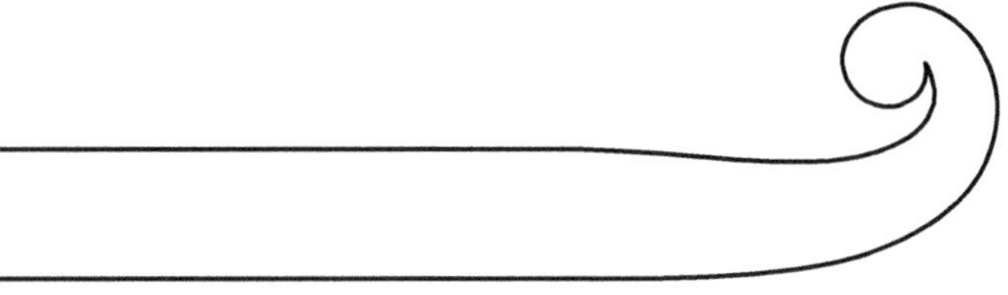

Minimal

The tail end of a serpent terminates in a single tightly curled spiral ball.

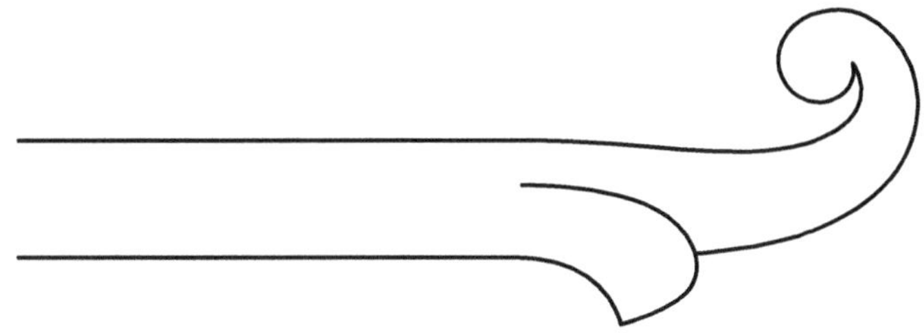

Classic

Curled serpent tail-ends are often accompanied by a lobe, creating a typical acanthus-leaf motif.

Body

Serpents are most often composed of a simple single ribbon, with the head terminating one end and the tail terminating the other.

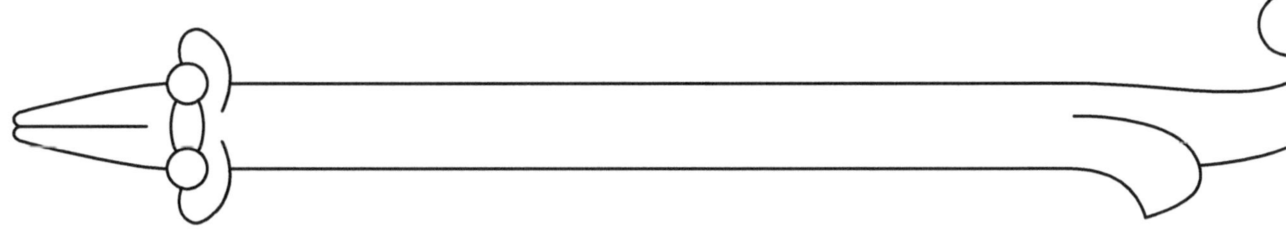

A full serpent composed of the head and tail connected by the ribbon body.

Beast Heads

Structure

The underlying structure of the head is composed of the overall shape (—), the flow of additional ribbon strands (—) and the main outlines of the head and its features (—).

General shape
- The outline of the beast's neck ribbon curls diagonally from the body and into a horizontal direction for the head.
- A vertical guideline marks the top of the ribbon's curve. The top outline continues straight to the front of the head.
- The bottom outline continues its curve, curling downwards.
- The front of the head is cut off diagonally to create the overall shape of the snout and jaws.

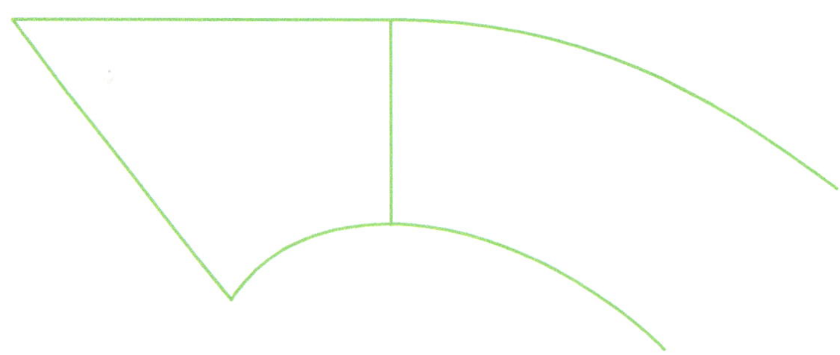

Facial Features
- Dividing the vertical line into four equal parts creates a guide for positioning the facial features.
- The almond-shaped eye sits approximately in the centre of the upper half of the ribbon.
- The back of the mouth begins approximately at the centre of the lower half of the ribbon.
- The lip of the lower jaw runs parallel to the curve of the bottom outline.
- And the lip of the upper jaw goes slightly upwards towards the snout from the back of the mouth.

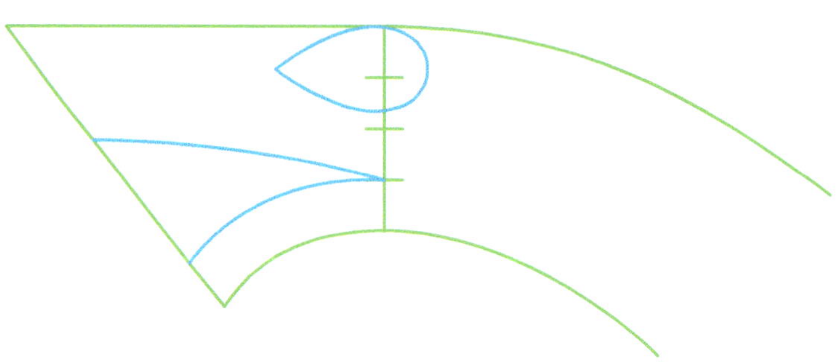

Ribbon Strands

- The lip-lappet ribbon strand curls around inside the outline of the snout and flows down in an S-shape just below and around the back of the mouth under the eye.
- The two teeth at the front of the mouth sit inside the outline of the diagonal end of the head parallel to the outline.
- The tongue strand rolls out in an S-shape from the back of the mouth.
- The crest's off-shooting neck-tendril strand continues the centre line upwards, bending at an angle just above the head.

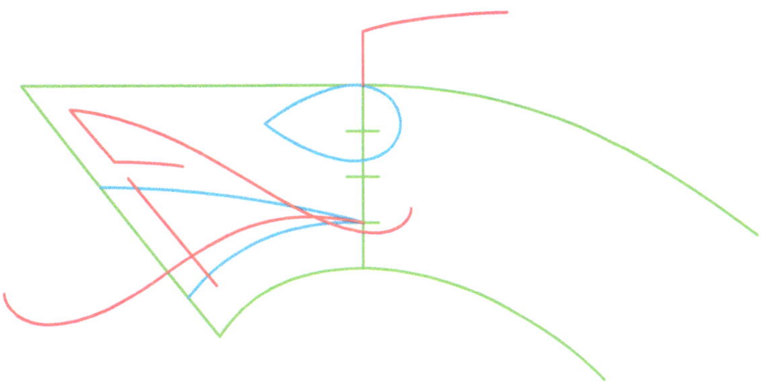

Crest

- The top contour of the snout and forehead are created by an S-shape curling downwards from the snout and ending in an upwards curve at the front of the crest.
- The neck-tendril ribbon shoots off from its base at the crest, going backwards from the top of the head.

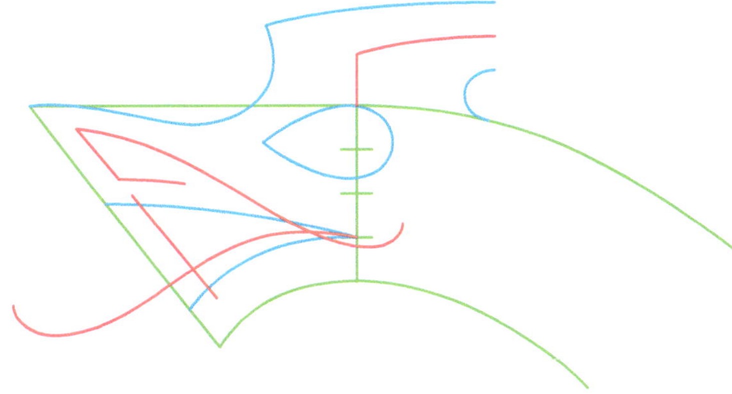

Rendering

The rendering of the head builds on the underlying guidelines, articulating the shapes of the facial features.

Eye

- The almond-shaped eye sits in the centre of the head.

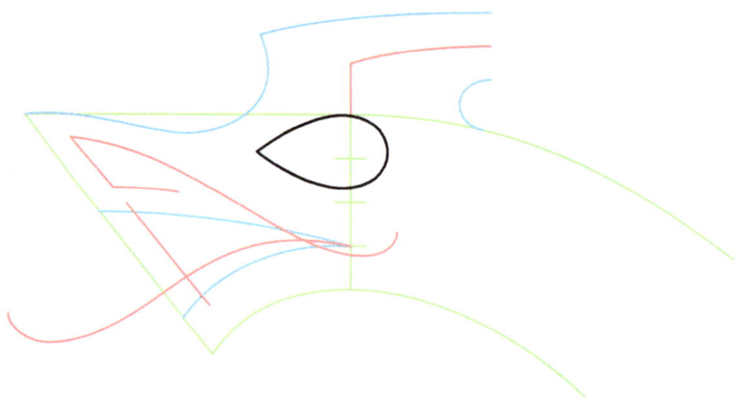

Jaws

- The outline of the upper-lip lappet creates the snout and upper jaw.
- The lower jaw is a simple ribbon rounded at the end, curling out under the lip lappet.

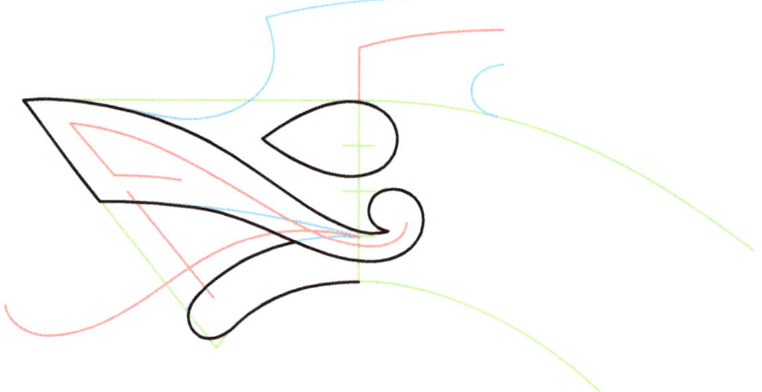

Mouth

- The two overlapping fang-like and almost almond-shaped teeth sit at the front of the mouth, each overlapping the outlines of the jaws slightly.
- Two lobes at each side of the top tooth create the gums of the upper jaw.
- The tongue rolls out from the back of the mouth as an S-shaped ribbon with a spiral-ball terminal.

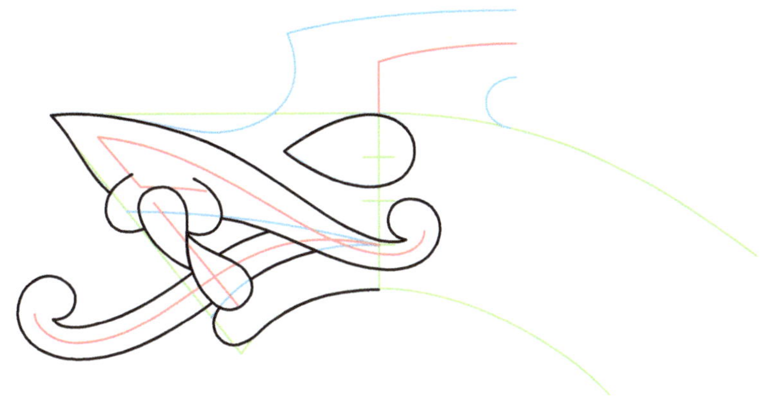

Crest

- The S-shape of the forehead terminates in two ear-like lobes sitting tightly together above the eye.
- The neck tendril shoots off behind the ears like a ponytail terminated by one or more acanthus leaves.

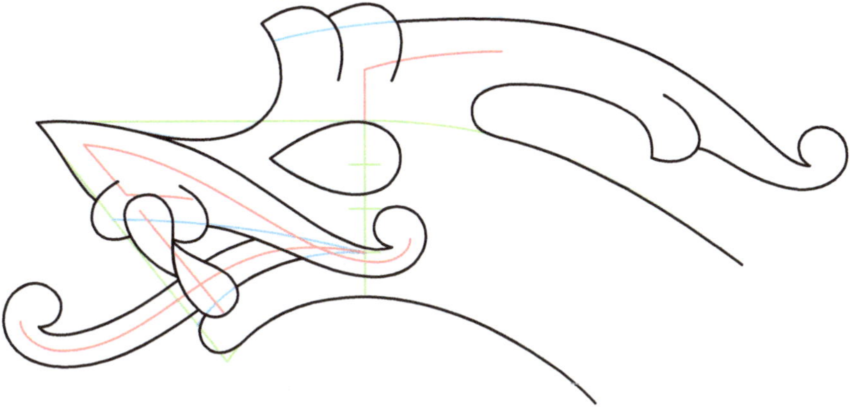

Beast Bodies

Structure

The underlying structure of the body is composed of the flow of its main ribbons (—) and outlines (—).

Main Lines

- The spine runs horizontally from the front hip's centre to the back hip's centre, often in a slight S-curve.
- The neck goes perpendicularly up from the front hip and curls around, going horizontally through the head.
- The thighs have smooth curves, the lower legs are almost straight, and the feet go straight forward from the ankle.
- The right side front leg is often lifted and bent at the knee.
- The knees of the front legs are shown here pointing forwards but can also point backwards like the back legs, which is a more natural position for the legs of a mammal.

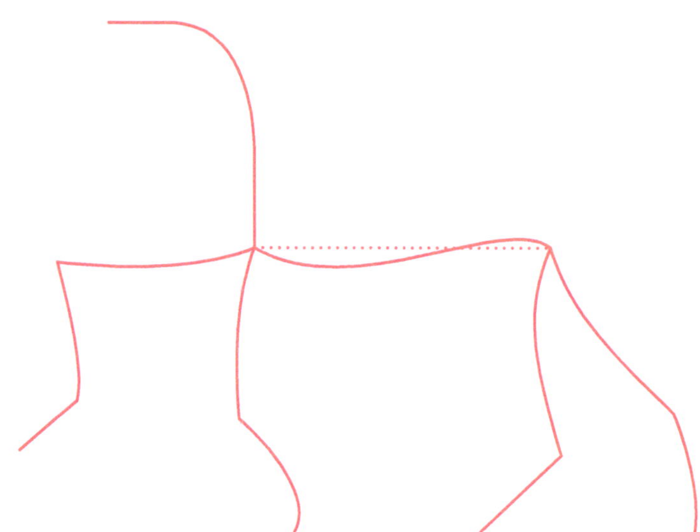

Hip Spirals

- The hips are composed of spirals facing outwards, beginning at the outside of the hip's centre point, curling around the midpoint once, ultimately flowing into the inner outline of the thigh, and continuing in a smooth S-curve into the lower leg.

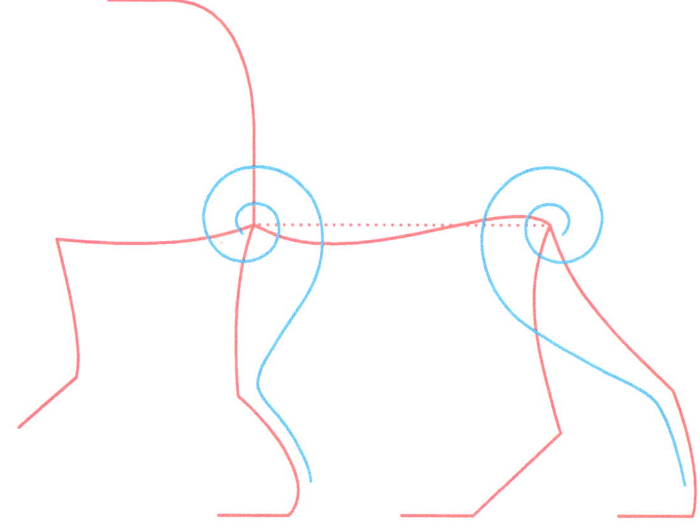

Triangular Thighs

- One line of the thigh's inner double contour begins where the spiral opens up into the thigh and runs parallel to the outline of the thigh down into the midline of the leg just before the knee.
- Another line runs parallel to the other side of the spiral, curling up over and into the bowel, where it fans out into a drop-shaped lobe following the curve of the inner side of the thigh.
- A third line goes in the other direction running down and into the knee, completing the triangular shape of the thigh.

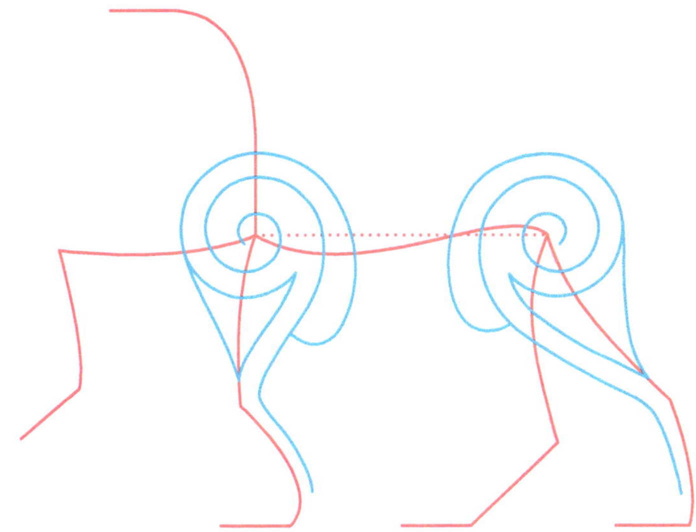

Left Side Legs

- The contour line of the outwards-facing side of the legs follows the flow of the leg and bends at the knee.

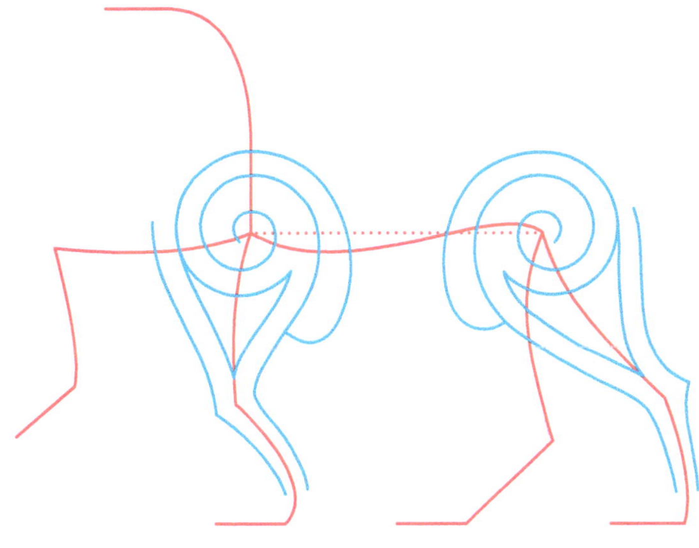

Body Contour

- The double contour of the neck follows the curve upwards and tapers into the head.
- The contour of the back and belly follows the flow of the spine's S-curve connecting the two hip spirals.
- The contour of the back continues the curve of the hindquarter before splitting off into the tail.

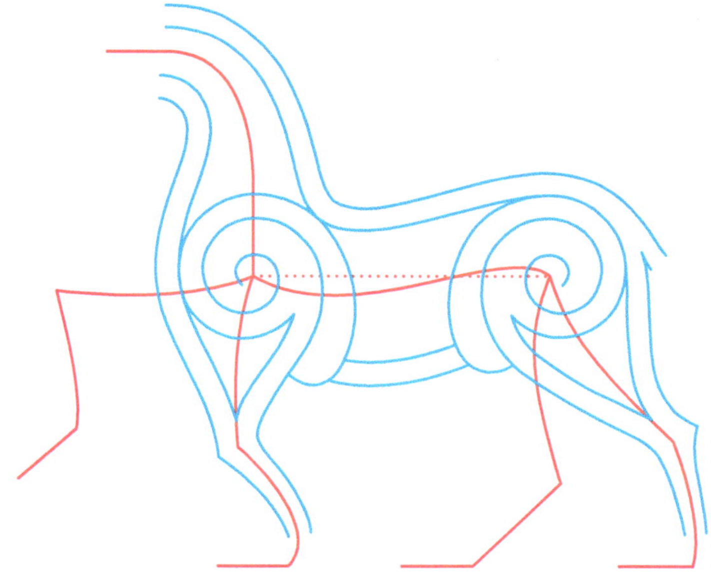

Right Side Legs

- The contour of the legs on the animal's right side picks up the width of the spiral thigh and tapers into the knee, bending into the lower leg.

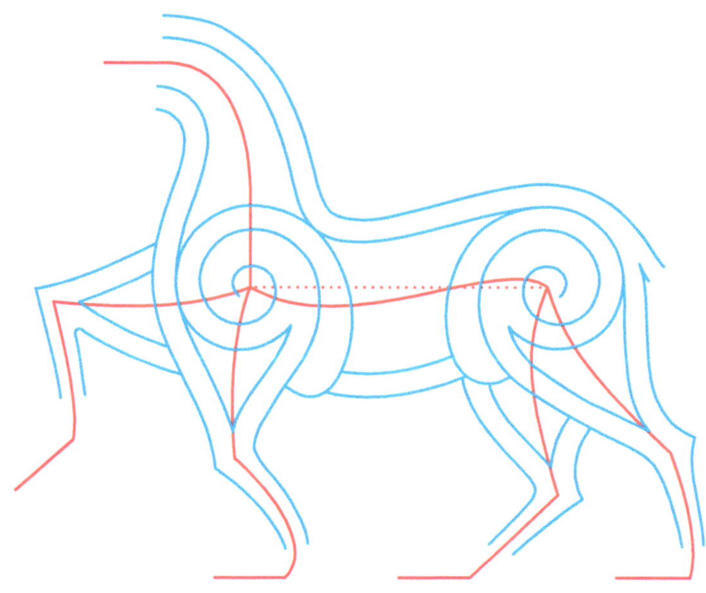

Rendering

The rendering of the body builds on the underlying guidelines, articulating the shape of the limbs.

Head
- The head continues the horizontal motion of the top of the curling neck.

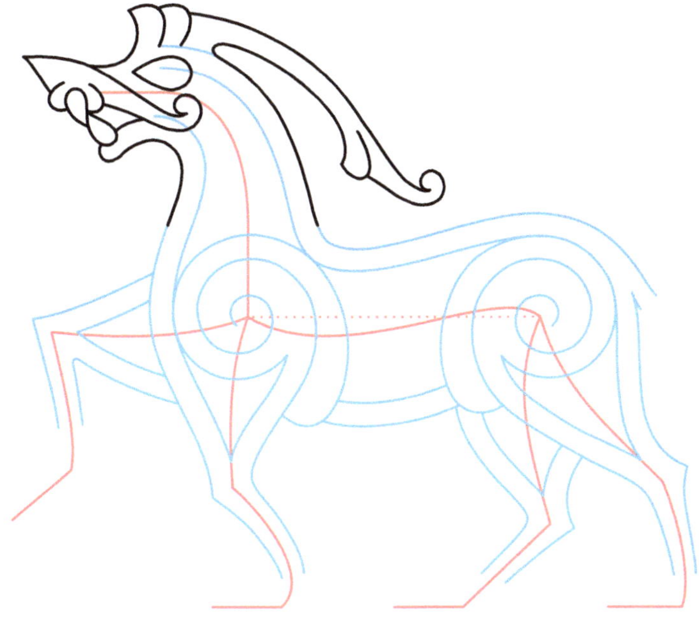

Tail
- The tail curls down, makes a U-turn and goes upwards in an S-curve above the back, terminating in one or more acanthus leaves.

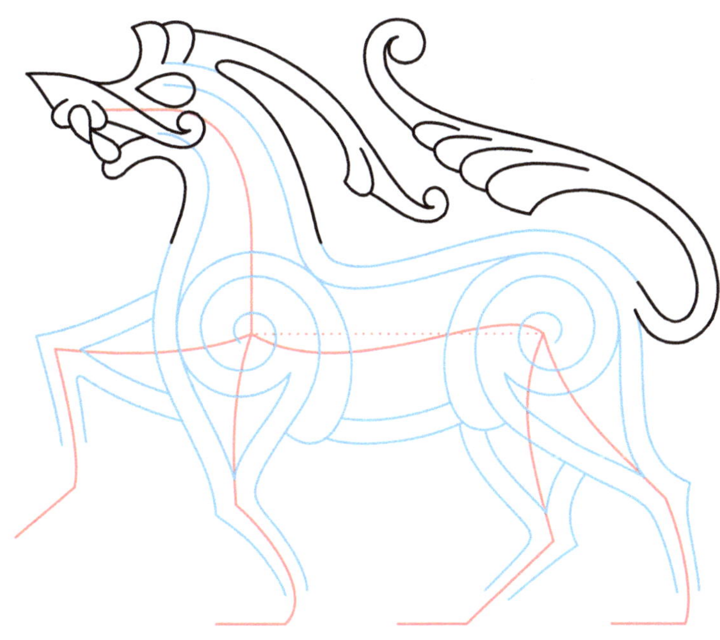

Feet

- The feet are triangular feline-like paws with two or three claws. A ribbon snippet accentuates the ankle joint, and a backwards-facing lobe sits right behind it like a hind toe.

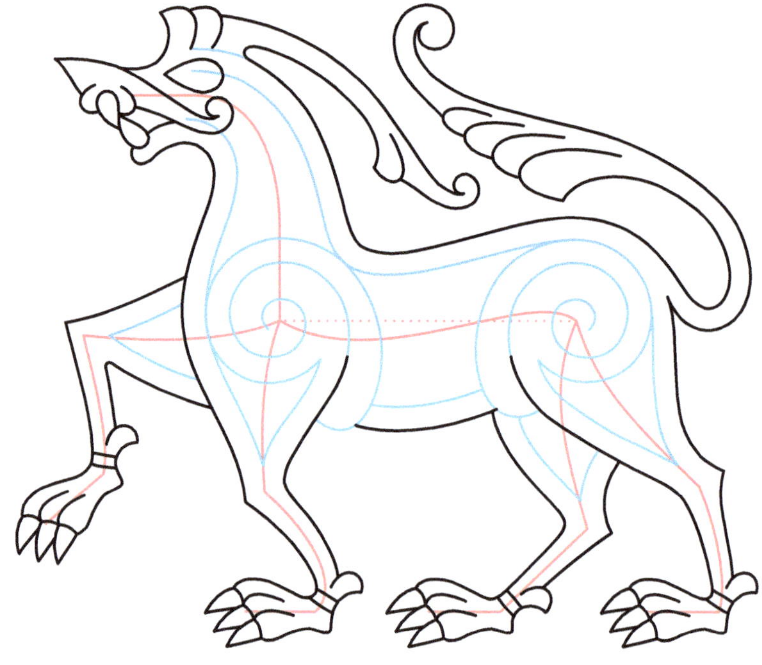

Knees

- A half-circle runs around the point of the knee cap inside the leg, emphasising the knee. And a ribbon snippet runs across the knee joint front to back.

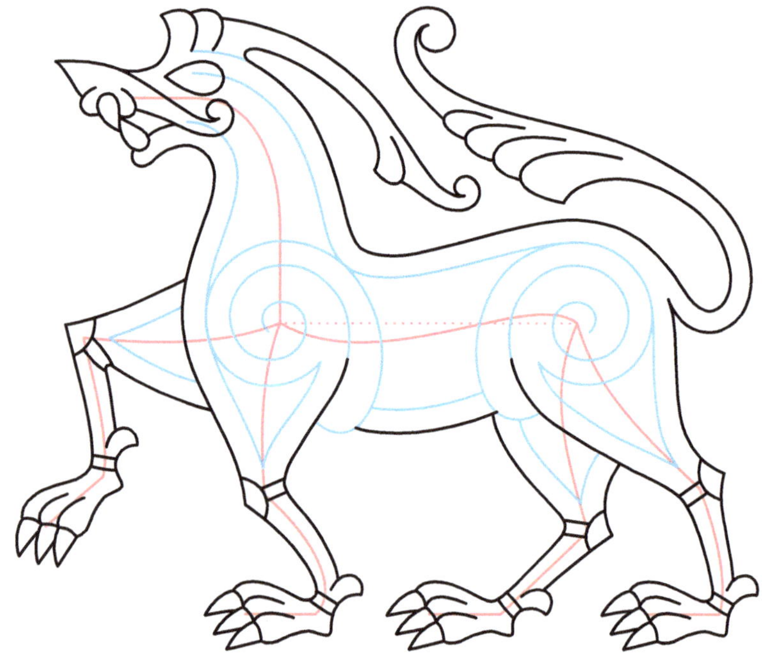

Hips & Outline

- The outlines of the legs run into the hip spirals, which have two or three large ribbon snippets beaming out from the centre of the hip, connecting the spiral ribbons and the outline of the body.

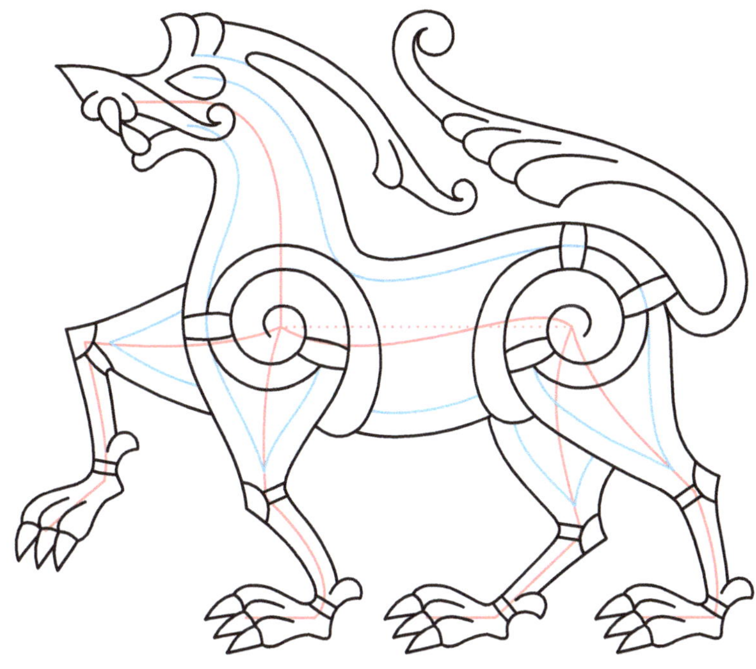

Double Contour

- The inner double contour lines run parallel to the outline of the body and limbs.

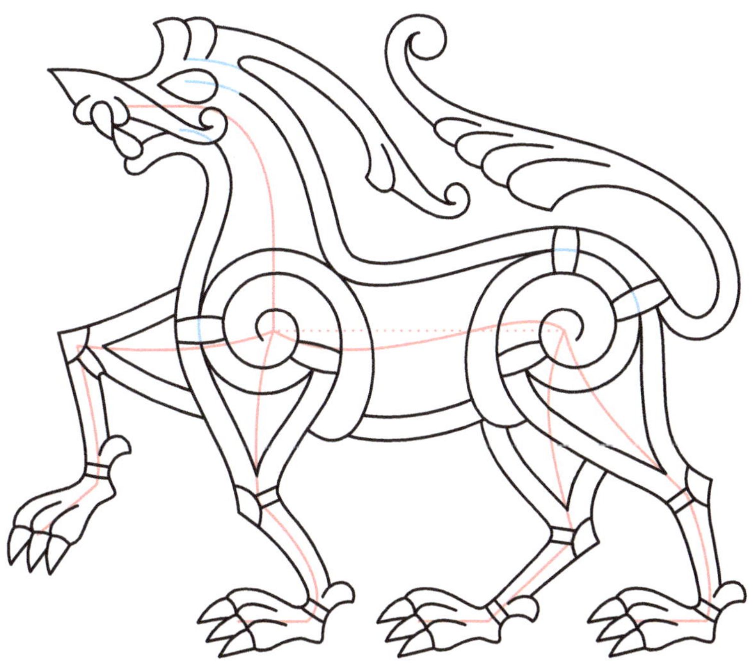

Ribs

- A few curvy lines hatched across the body often mark the ribs.

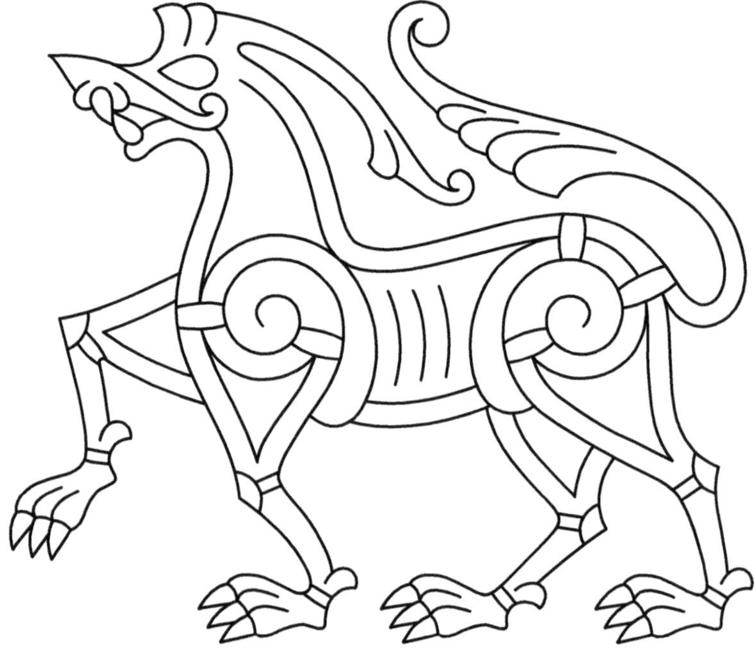

Alternative Configurations

Head Pointing Backwards
- The head can also be flipped horizontally across the vertical centre axis of the front hip, looking back over the body.
- The contour of the back then flows up into the neck and chin in a nice circular motion.

Tail Between the Legs
- Likewise, the direction of the tail can be flipped, going under the animal instead of above.
- Rather than making the U-turn, it continues the hindquarter's curve, curling around the hip's centre in a nice open circular motion down in between the hind legs and then up across the body, terminating above the back.

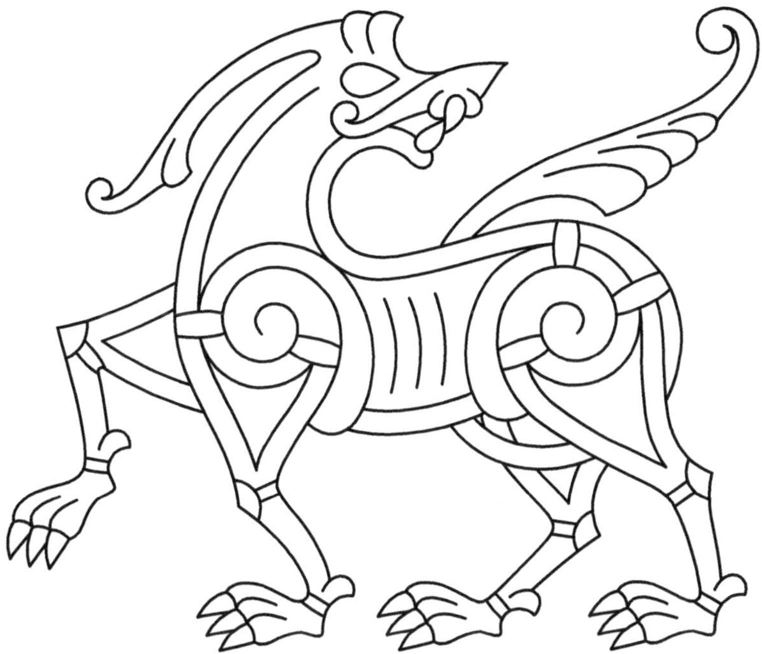

Knotwork

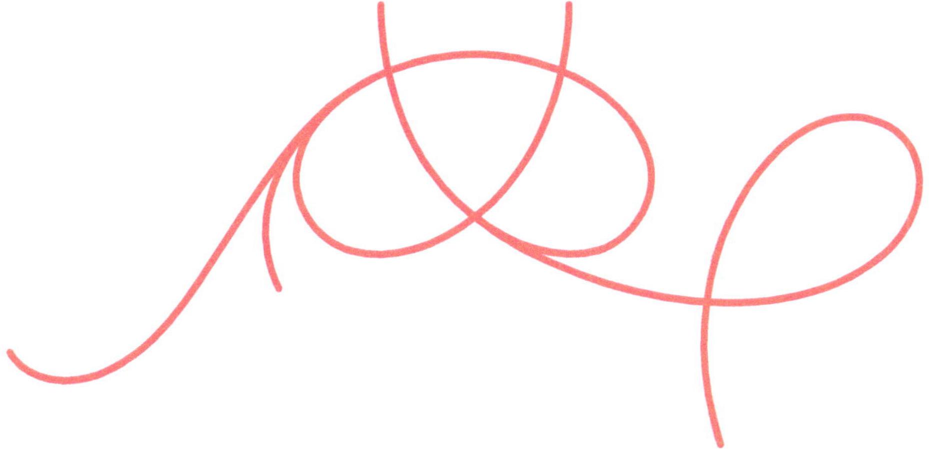

Loops and Knots

Ringerike-style knotwork patterns are composed of particular schemes of looping patterns and knots.

A select range of loops and knots are used on several compositional levels to create everything from the overarching main lines down to distinct details of the ornament.

Even mechanisms for sprouting the numerous tendrils creating the palmettes and multilayered knots are based on these principles.

Exercises

Take a look at the Ringerike-style designs at the back of the book. Can you identify the loop patterns, knots and offshoots described in the chapter? Try tracing the ribbon midlines one by one to deconstruct the structure of a composition.

Practice drawing the loop and knot patterns one by one. Try getting the curves as smooth as possible. When you're confident drawing the loops and knots, move on to practice combining different patterns to create more complex compositions.

Loops

The core element of a Ringerike-style knotwork pattern is a pear-shaped loop.

It might seem trivial to state this, as simple loops occur in all styles of Viking Age art. But in the Ringerike style, the pear-shaped loop is especially emphasised as an essential building block and compositional principle of the knotwork designs.

The pear-shaped loop is generally used in one of two ways; Either as part of a curly-loop pattern or a figure-eights scheme.

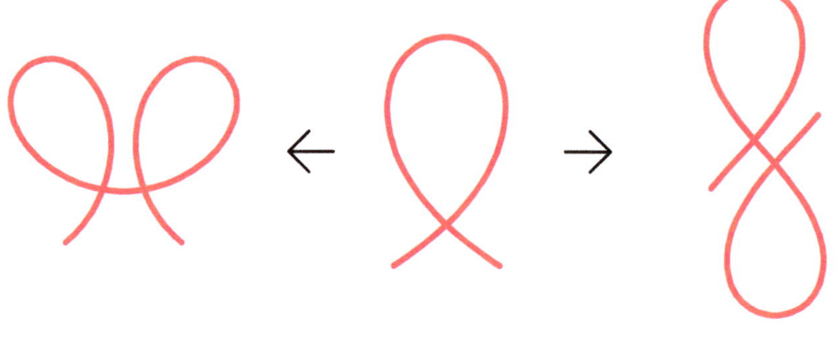

Curly loops   Pear-shaped loop   Figure-eight loops

Curly Loops

The curly-loop pattern repeats the circular motion of the loop curling in the same direction, creating a string of consecutive loops similar to a stretched-out spiral cord.

Curly loops are used extensively and indiscriminately throughout all Ringerike-style designs.

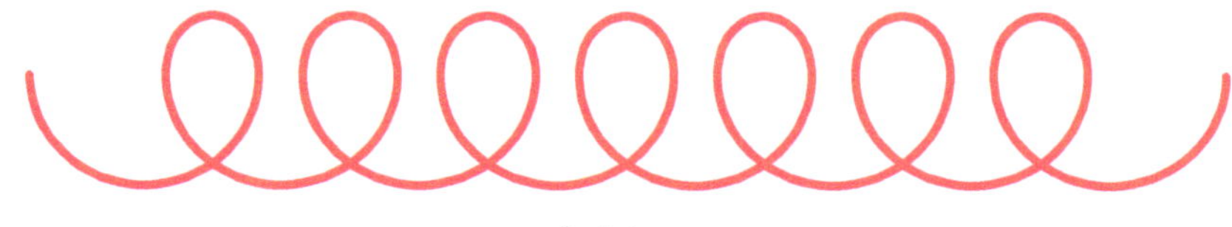

Curly loops

Figure-eight Loops

The loops of a figure-eight looping scheme, on the other hand, always curl in the opposite direction of each other.

Its structural function is varied, and it can feature as a simple minuscule interlacing mechanism repeated throughout a design as well as a central element drawing the main compositional lines. But it is most often used sparsely and selectively in a design.

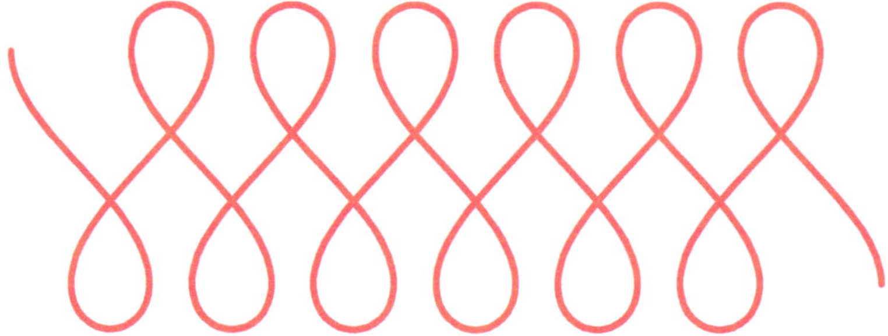

Figure-eight loops

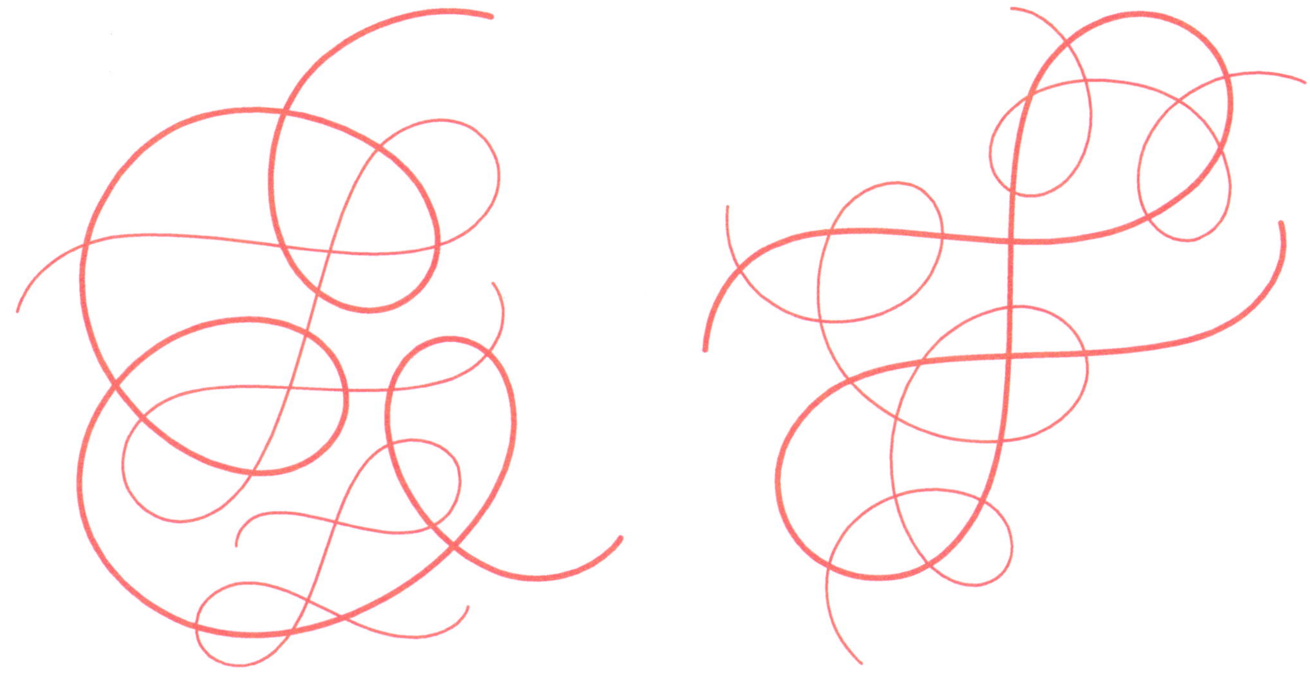

Curly loops with figure-eight loops

Figure-eight loops with curly loops

In Application

Figure-eight loops are usually limited to only two loops per ribbon, whereas there is no limit to the number of consecutive loops of a curly-loop ribbon.

Both types of looping schemes usually occur together in a given knotwork design. But they are virtually never applied to the same ribbon element.

Instead, ribbons with curly loops and ribbons with figure-eight loops mixed in a knotwork design are juxtaposed and woven into each other.

In other words: each ribbon always sticks to only one of the two types of looping schemes; either strictly curly loops or exclusively figure-eight loops.

Knots

The simple pear-shaped loop and the curly-loop scheme are essential for constructing the knots used in a Ringerike-style design.

The style's two most common knots, pretzel and triquetra knots, are effectively created by a curly-loop ribbon rotating its pear-shaped loops in relation to each other, overlapping and weaving them into each other.

The pretzel knot consists of two interlacing loops with open ends, while the triquetra knot creates a closed circuit by connecting the loose ends of the pretzel knot in a third loop.

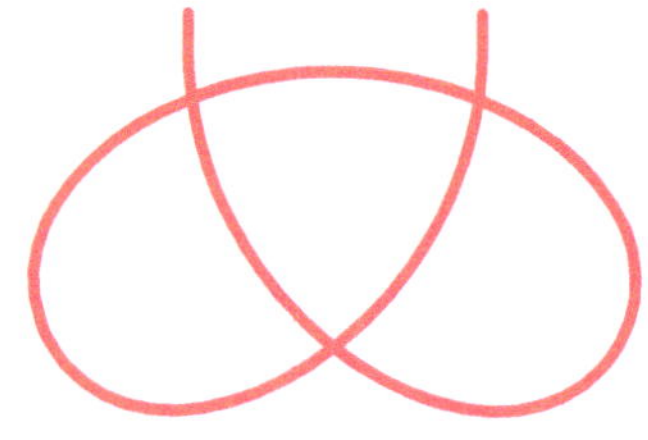

Pretzel Knots

The pretzel knot is by far the most common of the two.

The knot's open-ended nature plays well into the Ringerike style's ornamental mechanics and its preference for repetition and juxtaposition of ribbon elements.

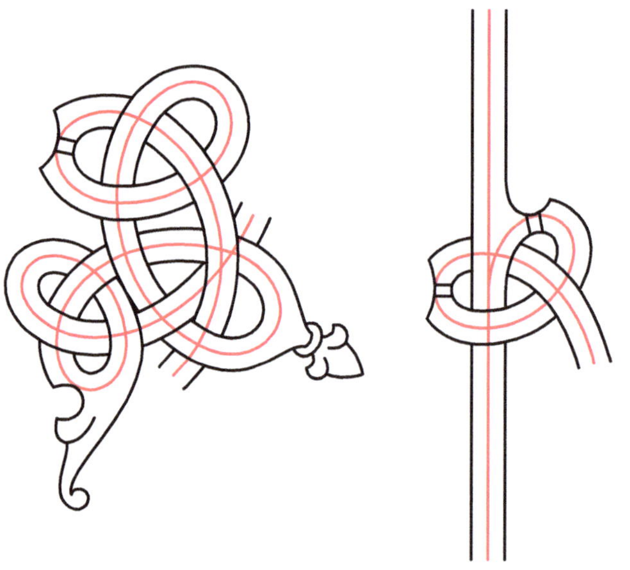

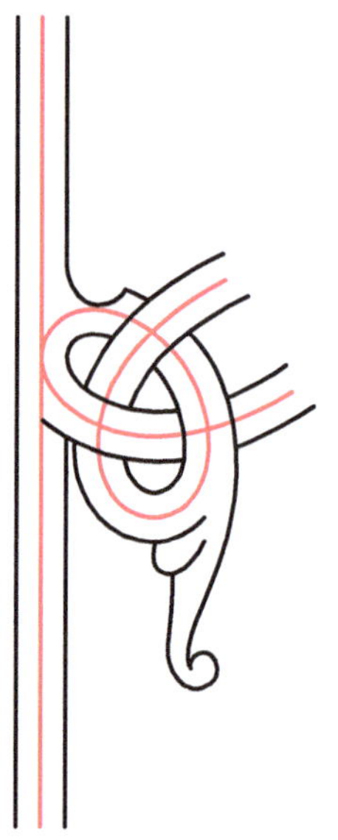

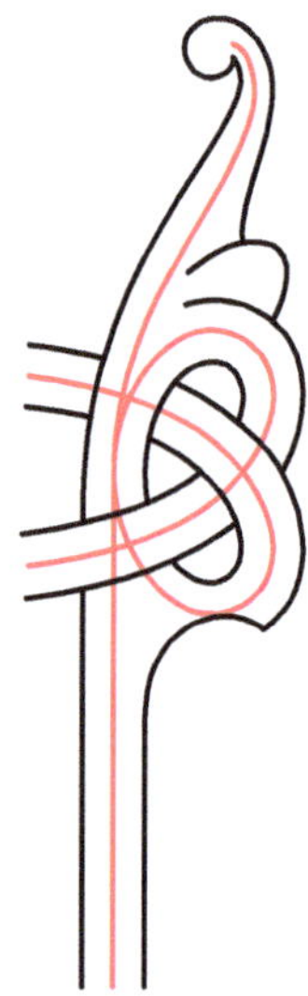

Free-flowing
The pretzel-knot scheme can occur free-flowing as part of a loosely woven composition, weaving in and out of other ribbon elements.

Offshoot
Forking out from a ribbon strand, the knot can act as an offshoot mechanism, adding additional tendrils to the knotwork pattern.

Base
Sitting on the side of a ribbon strand with the top of one of its loops connected to the main ribbon, the knot acts as a base for multiple tendril offshoots.

Terminal
The knot can also occur at the end of a ribbon, acting as a ribbon terminal, potentially creating additional offshoots.

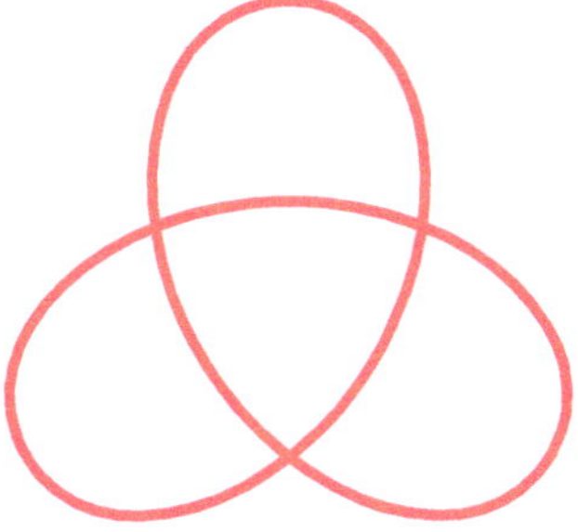

Triquetra Knots

Triquetra knots are used more sparsely and seem to be a leftover from the preceding Mammen style, where they are seen much more frequently.

But they do occur, especially in early Ringerike-style designs.

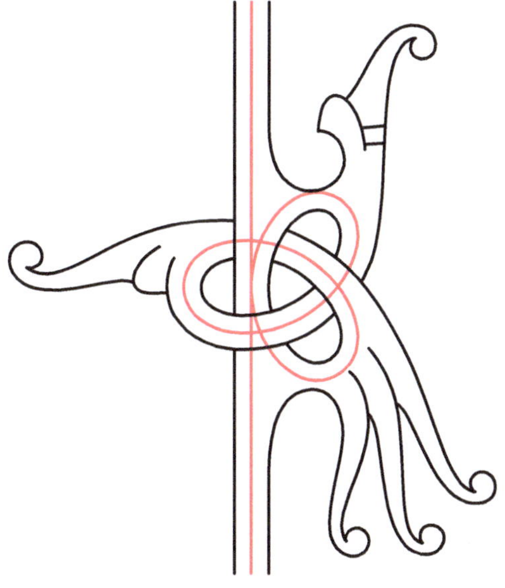

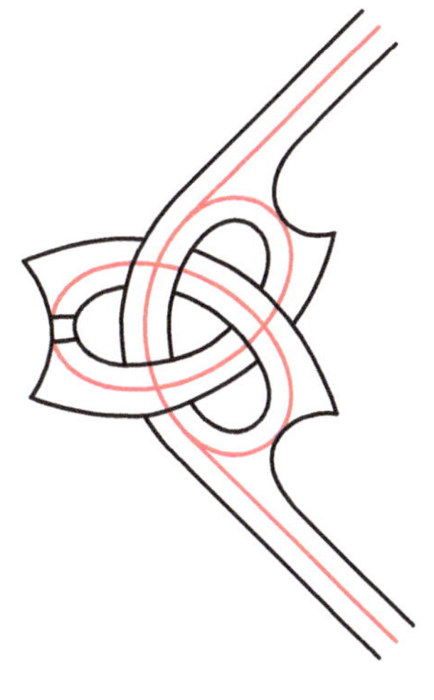

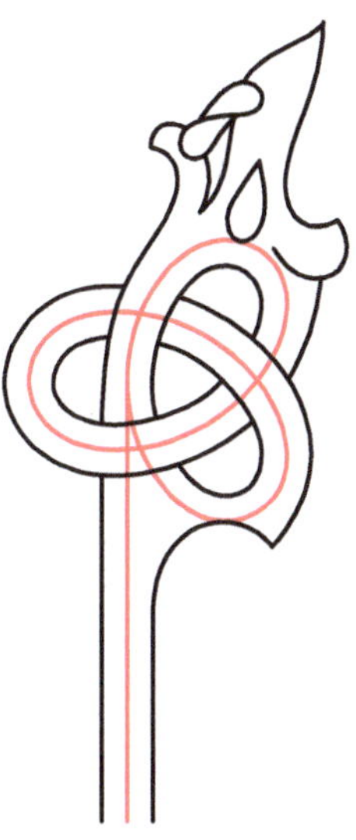

Offshoot
The triquetra knot can sit on the side of a ribbon, with the ribbon running through one of its protruding loops. The knot is attached at the top of one of its internal curves while tying itself around the ribbon. The loops can be used as mechanisms for foliage offshoots fanning out in all directions.

Corner
The knot acts as an elaborate corner piece by bending the main ribbon around the knot's centre at a 90° angle. This is a common way of applying the triquetra knot as part of a ribbon border running around the edge of a design framing the composition.

Terminal
Like the pretzel knot, the triquetra knot can act as a ribbon terminal, either in the shape of an animal head or by sprouting additional foliage and tendrils.

Double Pretzel Knots

The double pretzel knot is a knotwork element unique to Ringerike-style designs. It is far from present in most designs. But when it is used, it's virtually always a significant element, although usually underplayed.

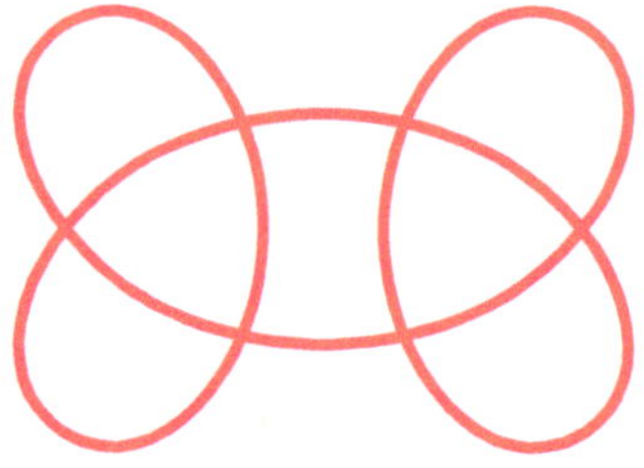

Double Knot

The double pretzel knot is constructed by mirroring a pretzel, connecting their otherwise open ends across the mirror axis at a perpendicular angle.

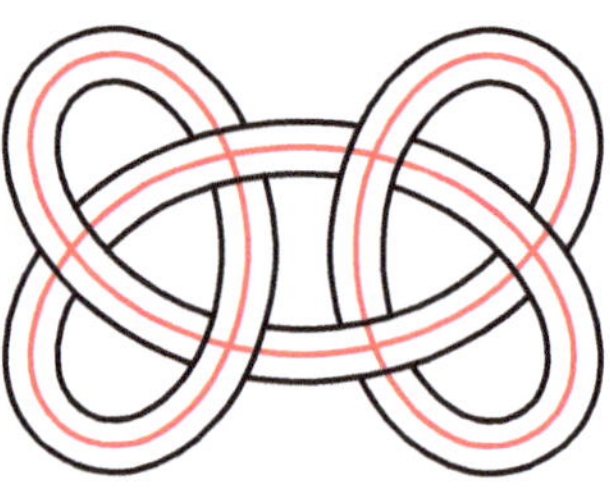

Free-flowing
A simple double pretzel knot can occur as a free-flowing part of a knotwork design, usually sprouting tendrils from its loops interlacing with the rest of the composition.

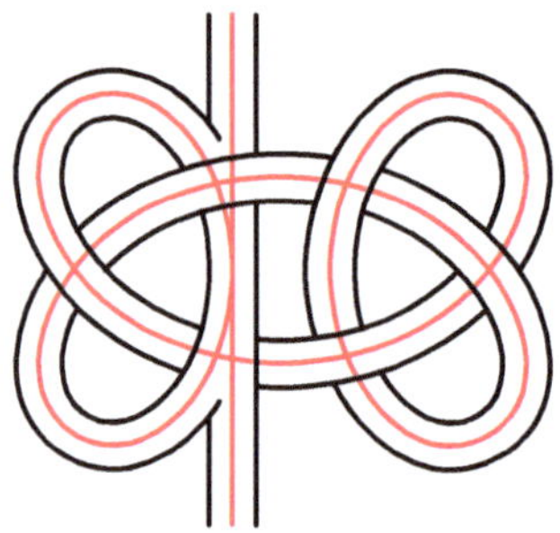

One Knot Attached
The double knot can be used as a sprouting mechanism by attaching the innermost curve of one of the pretzels to a ribbon running parallel to the mirror axis.

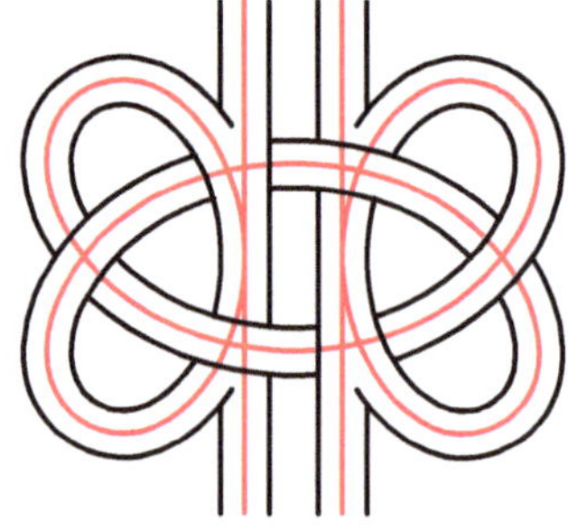

Both Knots Attached
Each of the two pretzels can also be attached to its own parallel ribbons.

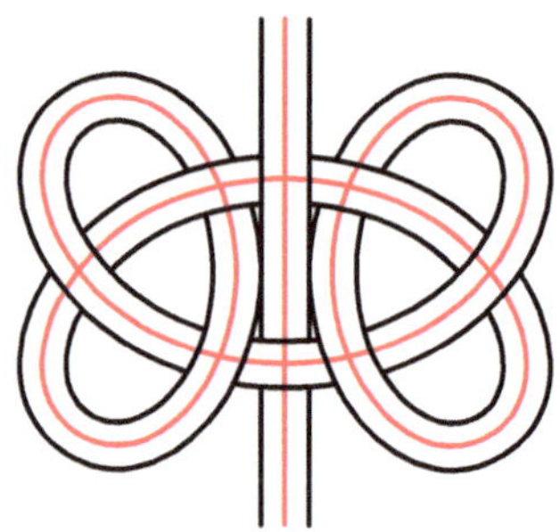

Tied
However, it can also be tied around a centre ribbon running along the mirror axis.

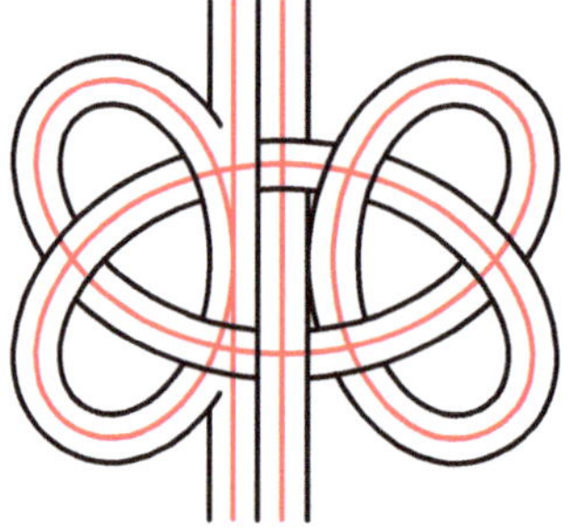

Tied with One Knot Attached
A centre ribbon can be added, running through the knot parallel to the attached ribbon

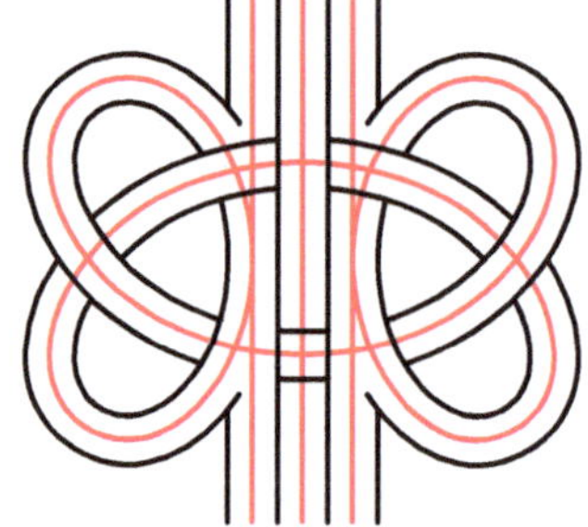

Tied with Both Knots Attached
A third centre ribbon can be added in between the two attached knots.

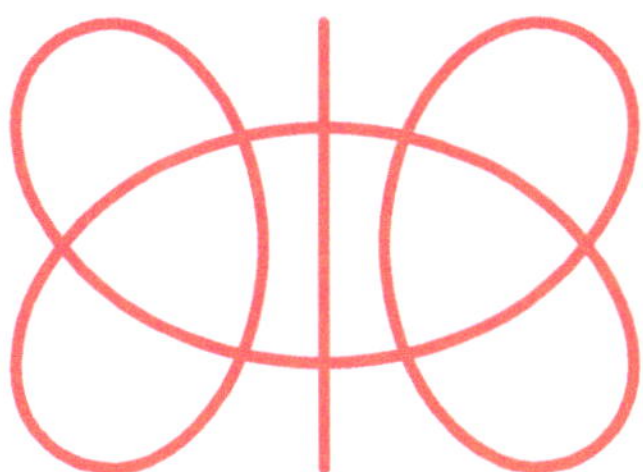

Tied Double Knot

A secondary ribbon often runs through the double knot along the mirror axis, with the two pretzels tied around it.

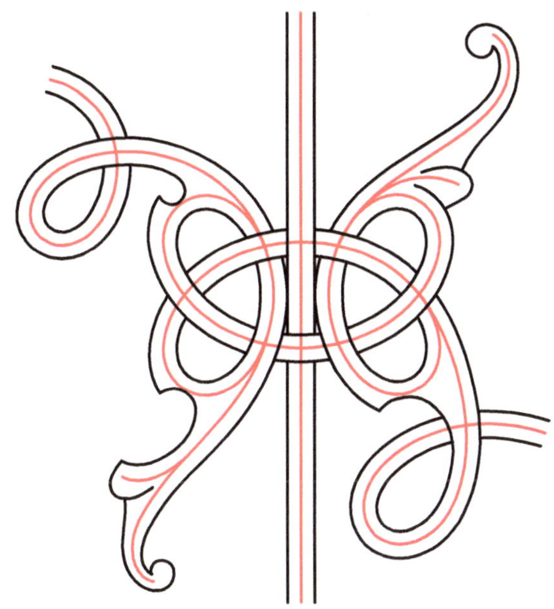

A double pretzel knot with offshoots tied around a centre ribbon.

Open Loops

The structure of the double pretzel knot can also work as an underlying guiding principle for constructing various knotwork patterns.

The knot's loops can be opened up in numerous ways to create open ribbon ends to extend, loop and interlace with neighbouring ribbon elements.

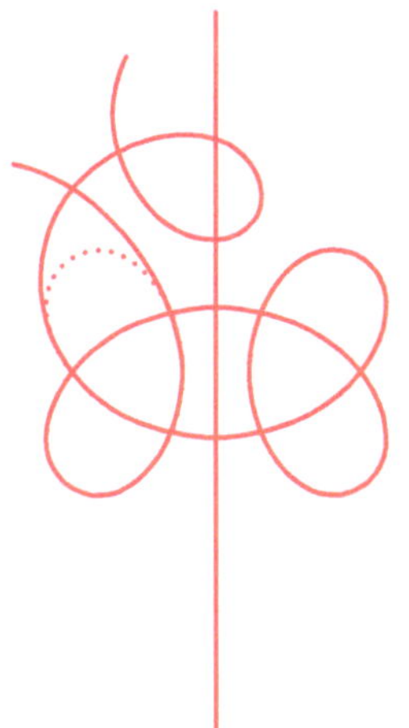

One Loop Opened
Only a single opened loop.

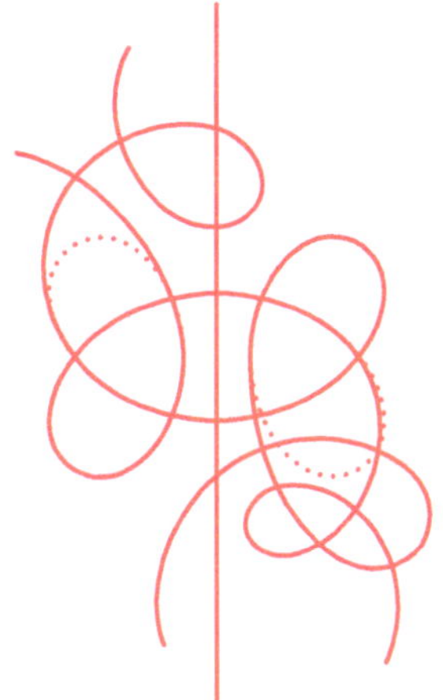

Opposite Loops Opened
Opened loops at opposite ends of the double knot.

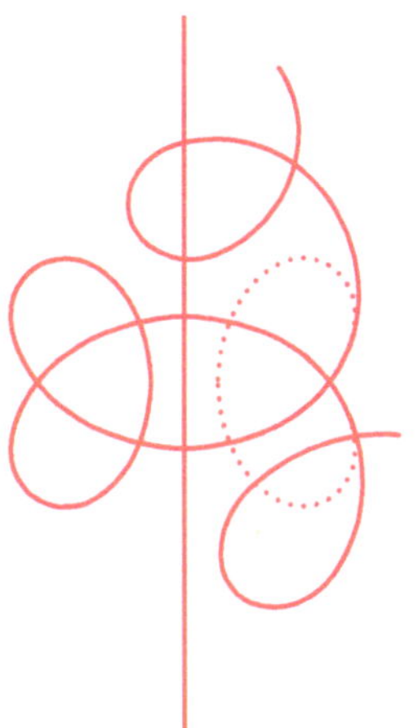

Same-side Loops Opened
Two loops opened at the same side and of the same pretzel.

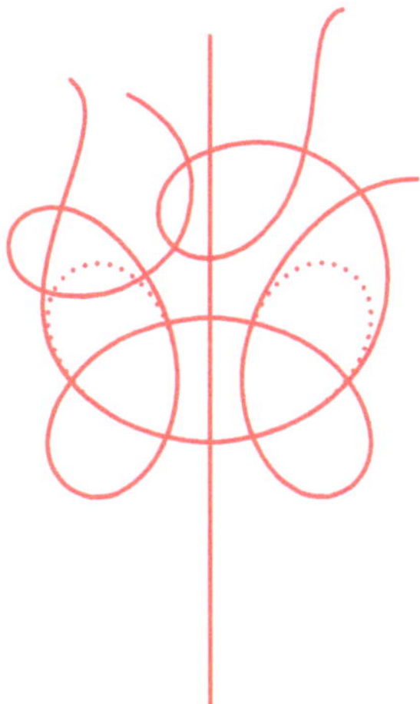

Parallel Loops Opened
Two loops opened, mirroring each other across the centre ribbon.

Offshoots

One of the Ringerike style's signature traits is its abundance of tendril offshoots.

The three essential mechanisms for creating offshoots in a Ringerike-style knotwork design are bifurcations, loops and spirals.

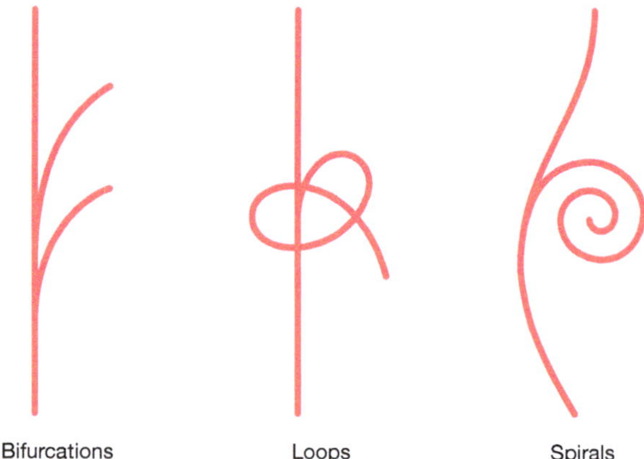

Loops

Loop offshoots are essentially bifurcations, but they behave differently than feathering offshoots with multiple bifurcations.

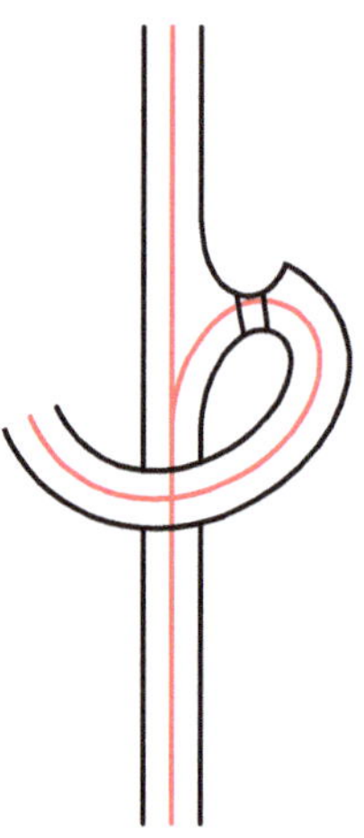

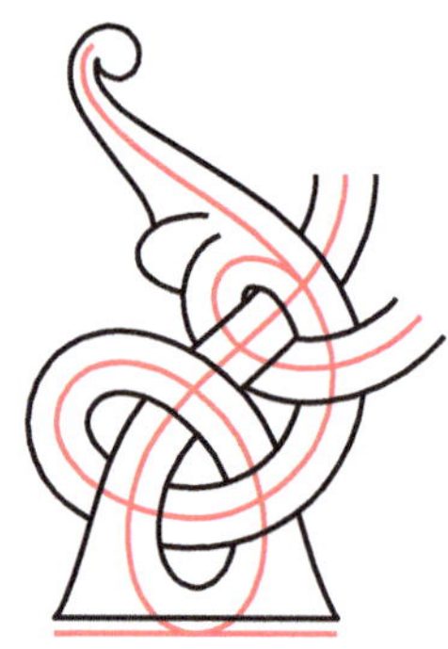

Loop Offshoots

A loop offshoot forks out from the stem and curls around and back, crossing the stem. The offshoot is often accentuated by a ribbon snippet, similar to the dented loop motif, and a dent in the outer curve picking up the outline of the stem.

Knot Offshoots

Multiple conjoined and interlacing loop offshoots create a knot attached to the stem. The ribbon stem forks out in opposite directions before tying the offshoots into a knot.

Knot as a Base

A knot can be used as the base of a stem, rooting the ornament to the edge of a composition, like a tree trunk to the ground. The outline of the attached loop flares out towards the base flattening out the curve of the loop, giving it an almost triangular shape.

Birfurcations

Bifurcations are the most straightforward way of creating offshoots. The offshoot simply peels off the ribbon stem.

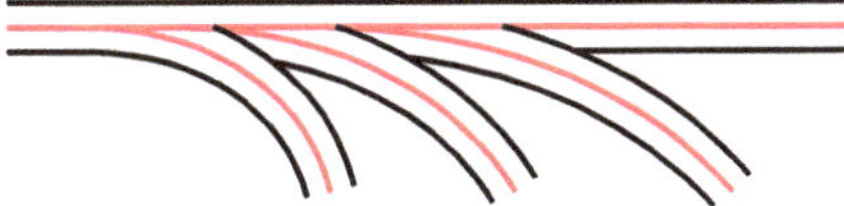

Feathering Offshoots
The ribbon stem forks into two or more strands peeling away from the main stem, like the barbs of a feather.

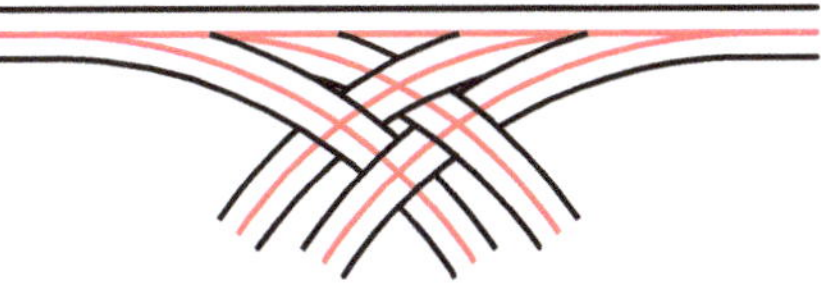

Braided Feathering Offshoots
A braided offshoot tuft is created by adding juxtaposed bifurcations in opposite directions, interlacing with each other.

Spirals

Spiral offshoots are distributed centrifugally along the ribbon curling inwards on itself. Ribbon snippets often cut across the spiral strand outside the spiral core, beaming out from its centre as if they are holding the coil in place.

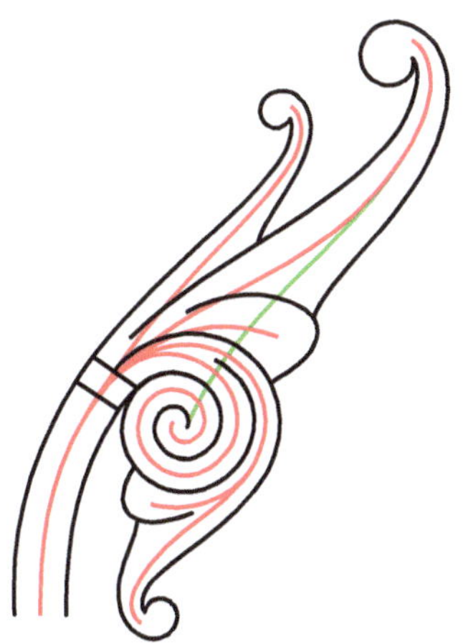

Spiral Offshoots
A spiral offshoot begins as a simple bifurcation curling in on itself, creating the spiral. Additional bifurcations around the outside of the spiral are distributed centrifugally, most likely in the shape of tendrils and foliage.

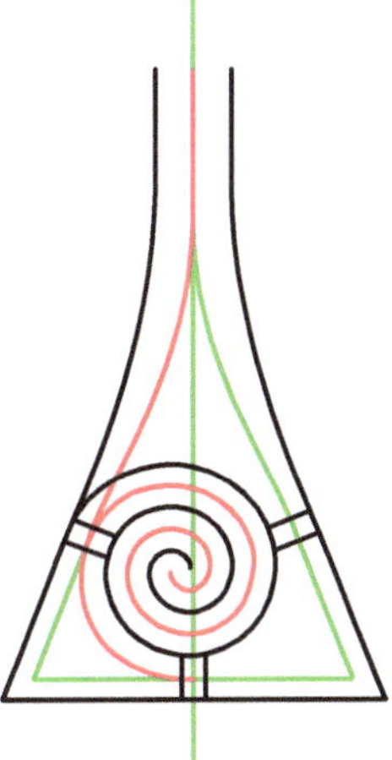

Single Spiral Bases
Spirals are often used as a base for a vegetal ornament rooting it to the baseline of a composition. The spiral curls up from the baseline inside the wide dovetail-shaped stem's bottom. Three or more ribbon snippets hold it in place.

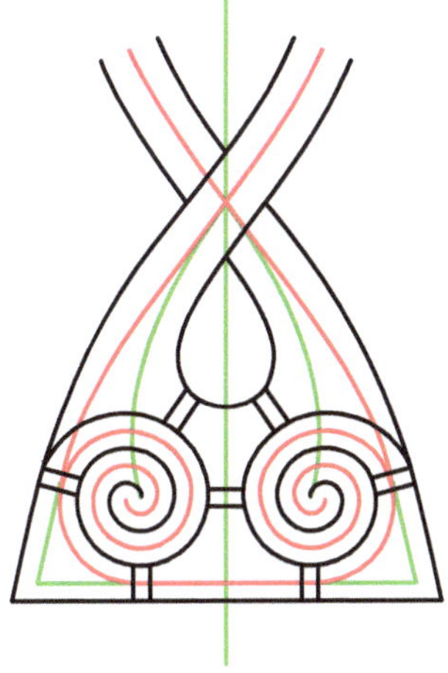

Double Spiral Bases
Two mirroring spiral bases connected by ribbon snippets are often used to construct the base of a symmetrical tree-like motif sprouting two twirling ribbon stems.

Knotwork-based Compositions

The main-line ribbons of a Ringerike-style composition are composed of a zoomorphic or vegetal element. Either way, the structure of the knotwork composition is built by a few hierarchical levels of interlacing ribbons.

A Beast Composing the Main Compositional Element

A large four-legged beast enveloped by serpents and vines is a common compositional motif.

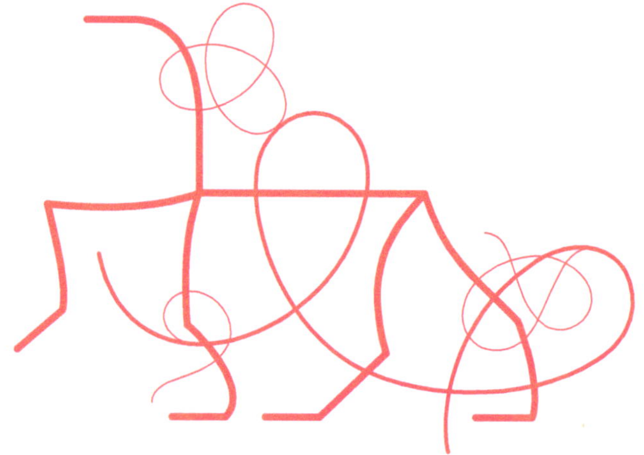

A Beast with a Large Curly-loop Ribbon
The secondary ribbon could be a vine or a serpent.

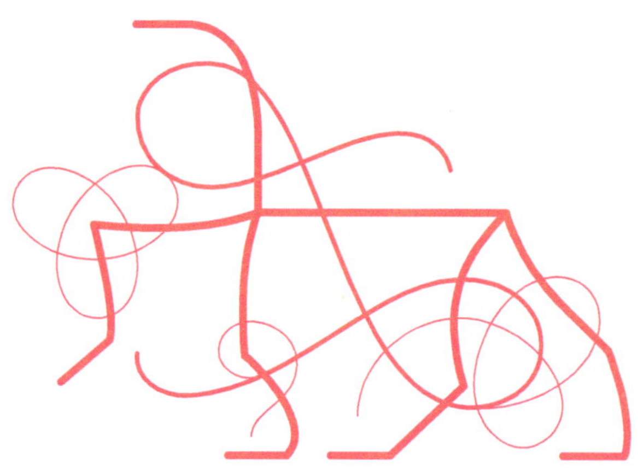

A Beast with a Large Figure-eight Ribbon
Large figure-eights are often in the shape of a serpent.

Primary Ribbons
The body and limbs of the beast compose the primary ribbons shaping the main lines of the composition.

Secondary Ribbons
A secondary ribbon element complements and balances the composition of the primary ribbons of the beast. The secondary ribbon is usually simple, composed either of a few curly loops or a single figure-eight.

Tertiary Ribbons
Various offshoots sprout from the primary and secondary ribbons. These are primarily strands of curly loops, pretzel knots and sometimes a triquetra.

Vines and Serpents Composing the Main Compositional Element

Pear-shaped loops are often used as the backbone of vegetal-based compositions or designs featuring large serpents as the central motif.

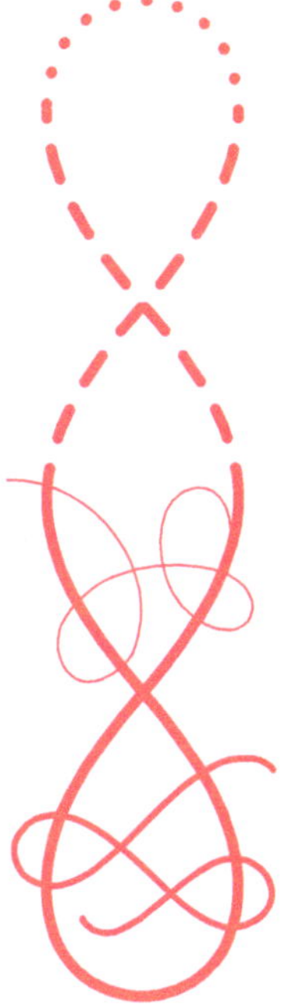

A Single Loop
The main lines are composed of large serpents or tree-like vines with twirling branches at the top mirroring the bottom loop.

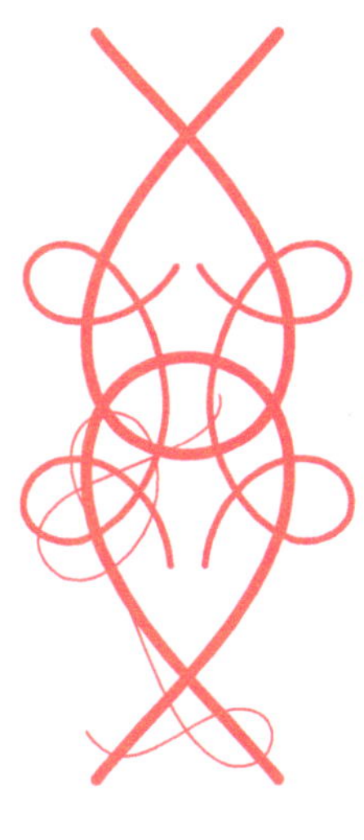

Two Overlapping Loops
Often in the shape of two serpents creating the symmetrical main lines.

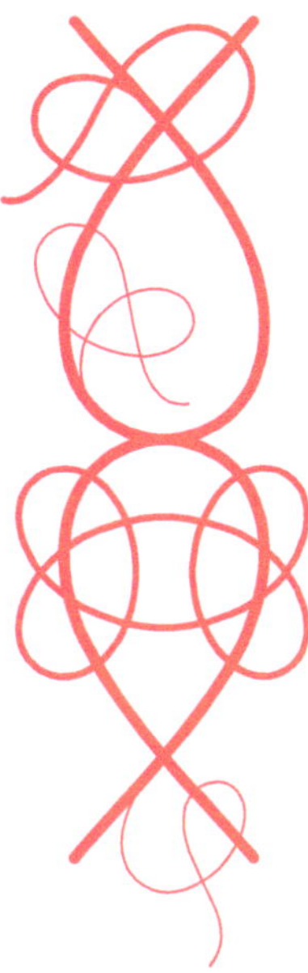

Two Connected Loops
Often in the shape of vines shooting out from the centre, creating the symmetrical main lines.

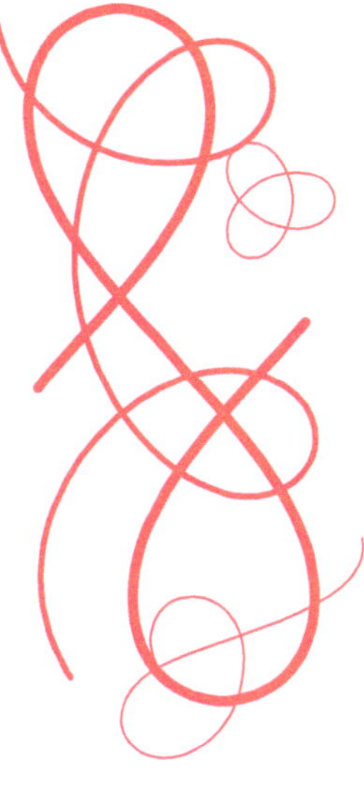

A Single Figure-Eight
Two opposing loops balance each other in rotational symmetry, usually in the shape of a large serpent.

Primary Ribbon
Main lines create balance through mirror or rotational symmetry.

Secondary Ribbons
A select few simple secondary ribbons loop around the stems of the main ribbon, either enhancing the symmetry or deliberately breaking with it.

Tertiary Ribbons
Various offshoots sprout from the primary and secondary ribbons. These are primarily strands of curly loops, pretzel knots and sometimes a triquetra.

Motif Variations

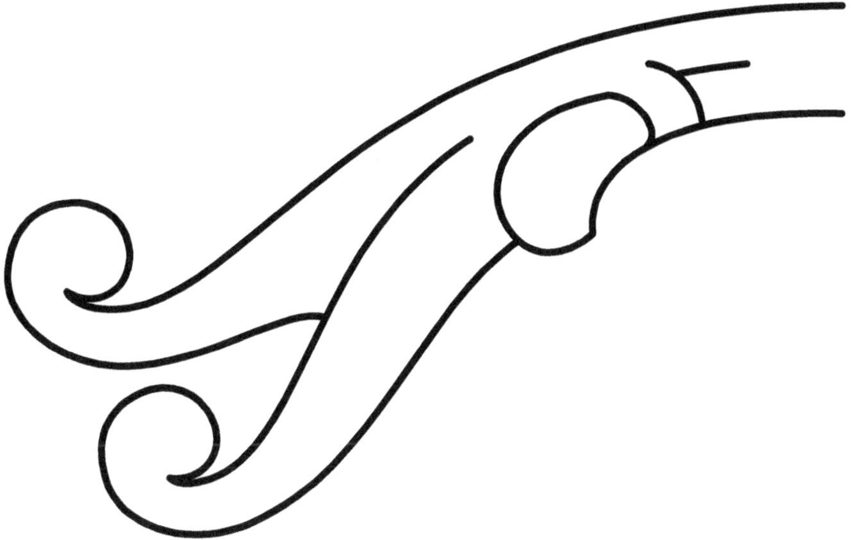

Reconfiguring the Core Features

An abundant and varied design is created by reconfiguring the fundamental ornamental motifs and knotwork patterns.

To create the intricate designs typical for the Ringerike style, several simple building blocks and design principles are combined repeatedly in numerous constellations to create the multilayered knotwork ornaments.

The core building blocks like acanthus leaves and pretzel knots can be reconfigured infinite ways using the essential Ringerike style principles to create customised and elaborate designs.

Exercises

Take a look at the Ringerike-style designs at the back of the book. Can you identify the variations of motifs and features described in the chapter?

Try recreating the motif variations. Select an ornamental motif and sketch as many variations of it as possible. You can also randomly pick two different motifs and combine them in various ways.

Acanthus Leaves

Forward-facing Lobe

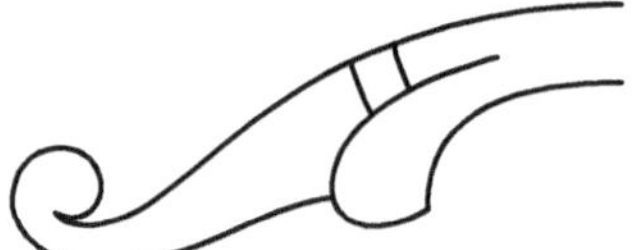

Basic Shape
The most common version of the leaf motif is composed of a squat lobe and an elongated leaflet curling up into a spiral-ball terminal.

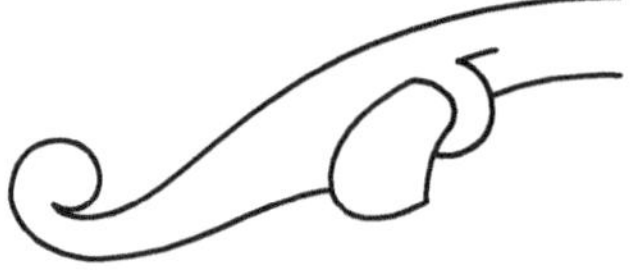

Ribbon Snippet
A ribbon snippet crossing the leaflet right next to the lobe is common.

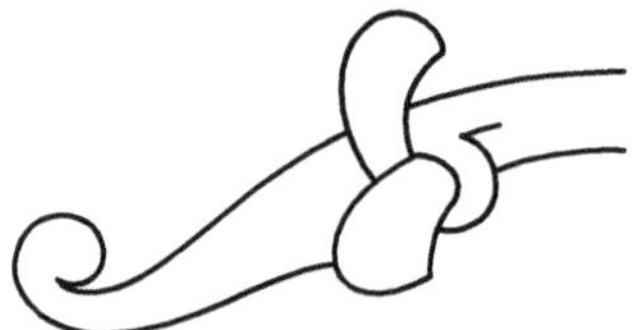

Curling Offshoot
The lobe is sometimes wrapped by a curling offshoot peeling off the leaflet in a backwards direction.

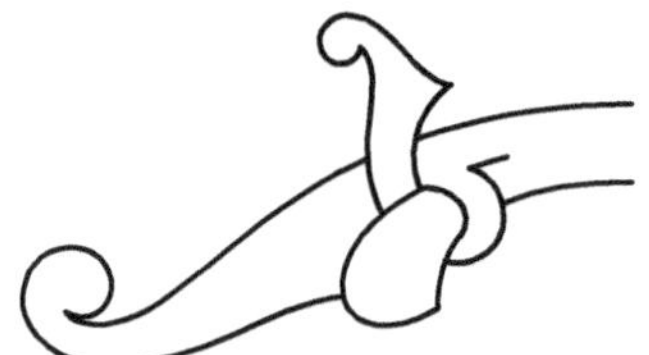

Curling Lobe
The curling offshoot is often terminated by a smaller lobe coming up in between the leaflet and the lobe.

Curling Leaf
The curling lobe can even take the shape of an acanthus leaflet.

Backwards-facing Lobe

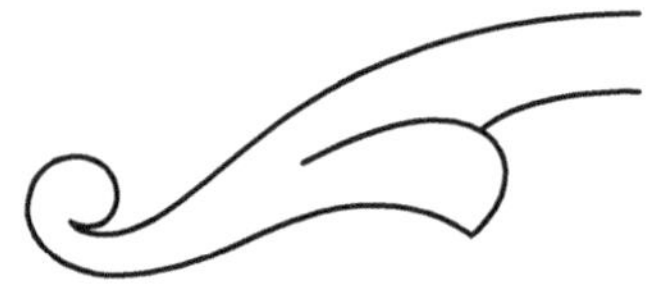

Basic Shape
The direction of the acanthus leaf's lobe can be flipped, turning the lobe backwards.

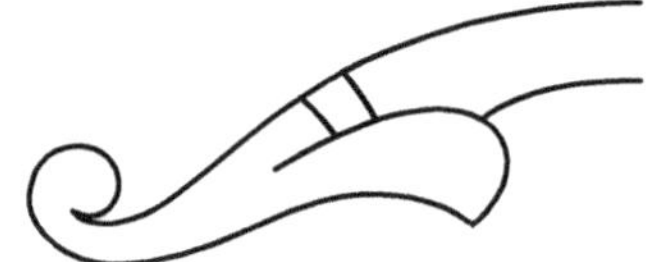

Ribbon Snippet
A ribbon snippet crossing the leaflet right next to the lobe is also common for this variation.

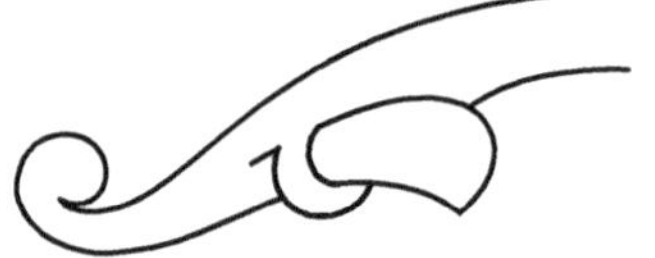

Curling Offshoot
Curling offshoots around a backwards-facing lobe peel off in the opposite direction.

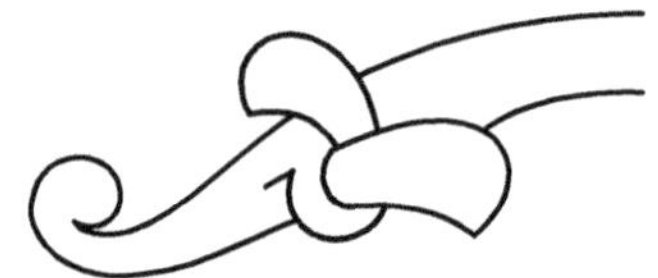

Curling Lobe
The smaller lobe is mirrored compared to the acanthus leaf with a forward-facing lobe.

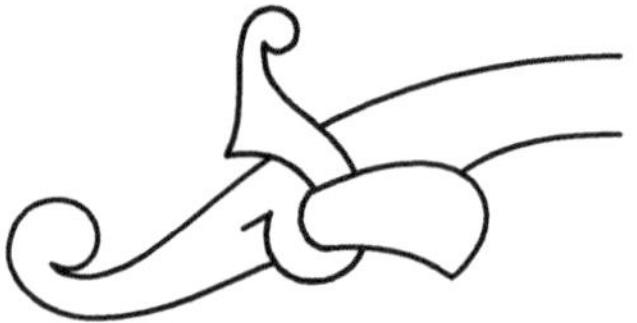

Curling Leaf
The leaflet is also mirrored compared to the acanthus leaf with a forward-facing lobe.

Multi-lobe Leaves

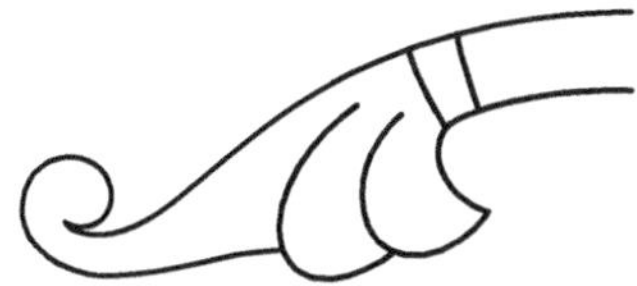

Extra Lobe
One or more lobes can be added just behind the first lobe in a feathering manner.

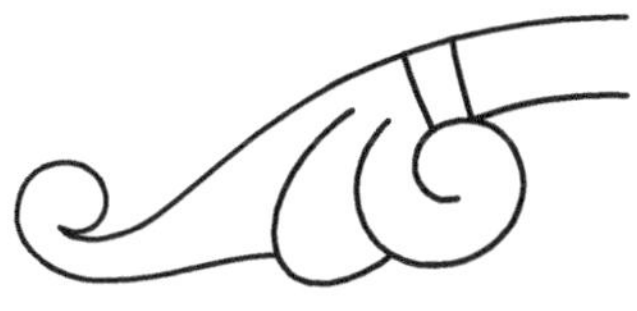

Spiral
A spiral can be added just behind the first lobe. A ribbon snippet sitting at the base of the leaf perpendicular to the spiral is common.

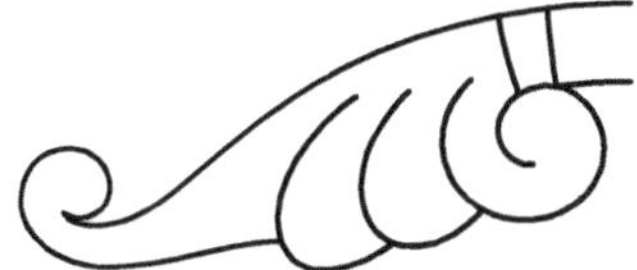

Extra Lobe and Spiral
The extra lobe and spiral variations can be combined.

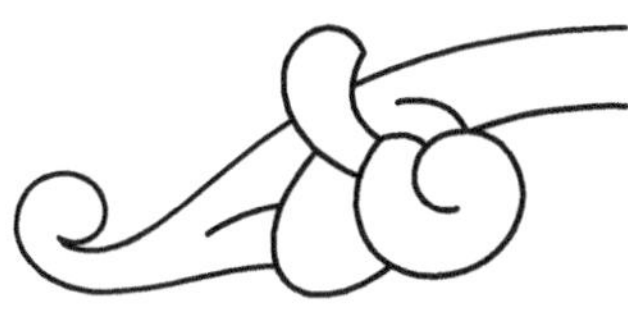

Extra Lobe and Spiral with Offshoot
The curling lobe can be added to the extra lobe and spiral variation, curling around the spiral's ribbon.

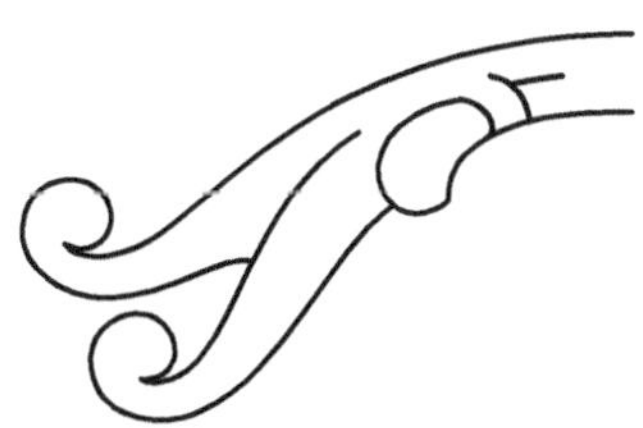

Extra Leaflet
The leaflet can be split into two or more strands.

Further Variations

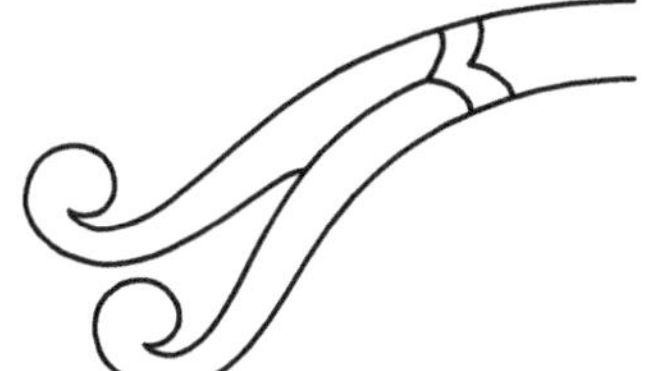

Double Leaflet with V-shaped Snippet
Turning the lobe into a second leaflet turns an acanthus leaf into a simple half-palmette.

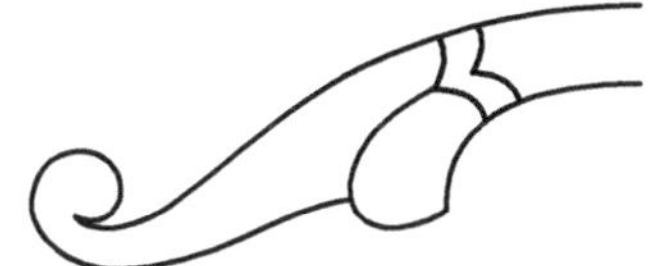

Forward-facing Lobe with V-shaped Snippet
The V-shaped snippet occurs on acanthus leaves too.

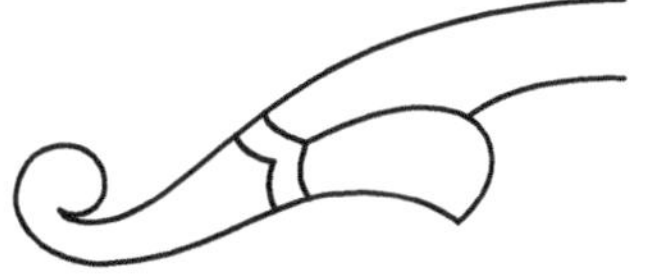

Backwards-facing Lobe with V-shaped Snippet
The V-shaped snippet is flipped on acanthus leaves with backwards-facing lobes.

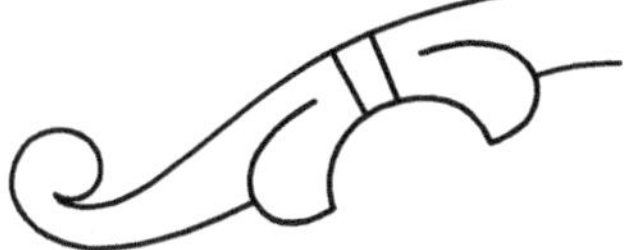

Two Countering Lobes
A backwards-facing lobe sitting right behind the forwards-facing lobe with a snippet in between creates yet another variation.

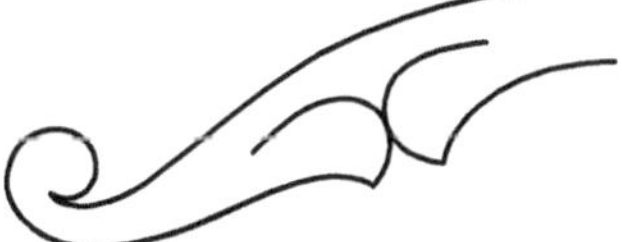

Two Facing Lobes
The lobes can also be facing each other. The snippet in between the lobes is discarded in this variation.

Union Knots

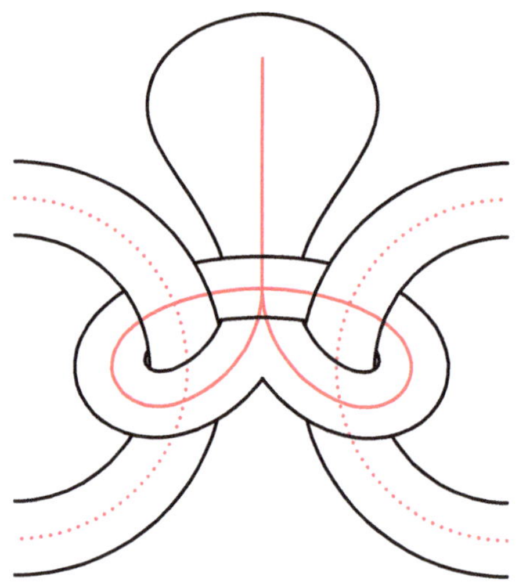

The union knot consists of two parts, the main ribbon composing the knot and two flanking ribbons tied into the knot.

The main ribbon begins as a straight vertical line splitting into two strands towards the bottom, each curling in opposite directions before rejoining again at the centre, crossing the vertical ribbon end. The loops curl around the two adjacent ribbons of the ornament.

The union knot can be flipped vertically, either facing upward or downward.

Upward-facing

The upward-facing end of the vertical strand terminates in a main centre lobe with two adjacent ribbons tied into the loops on each side.

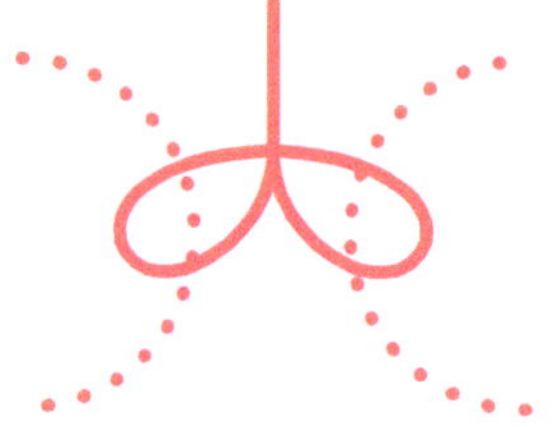

Downward-facing

Turning the knot upside down, the centre lobe now sits on top of the two loops connected to the main lobe by an opening in the outline where the ribbon splits in two.

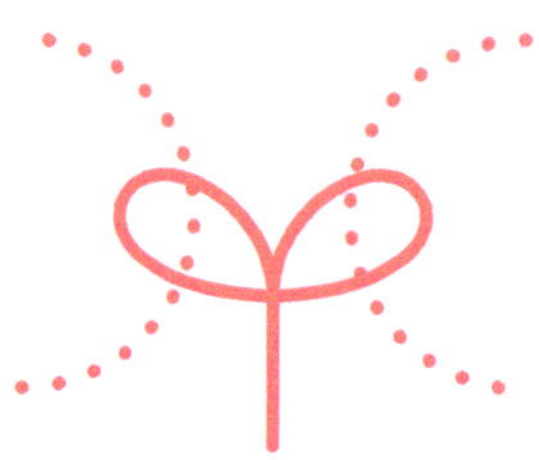

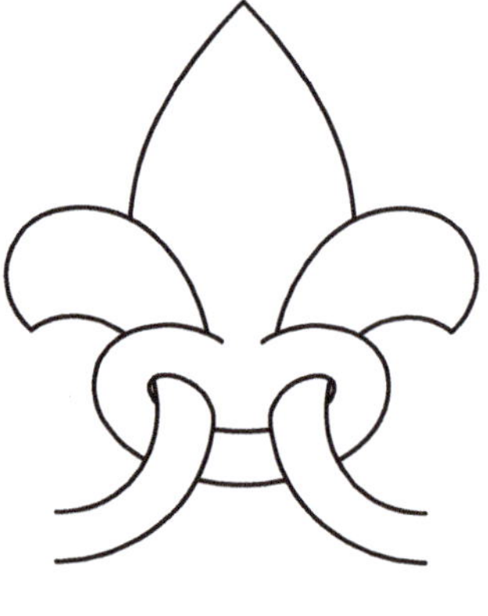

Top Centre Lobe
The union knot connects two loose ribbons wrapping them up into the knot.

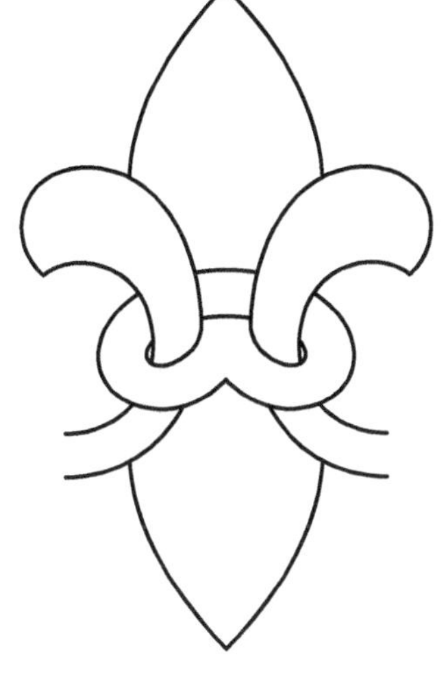

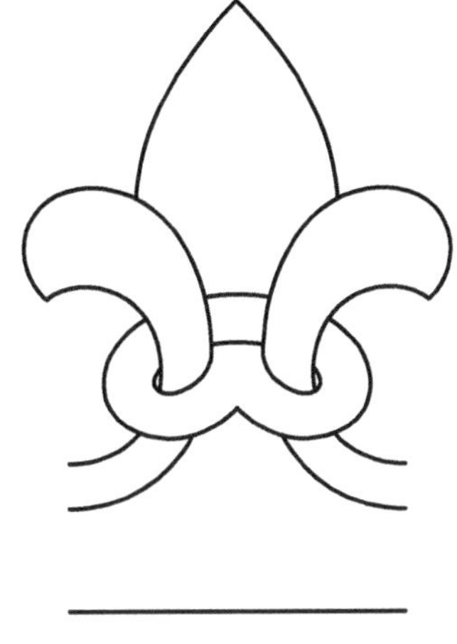

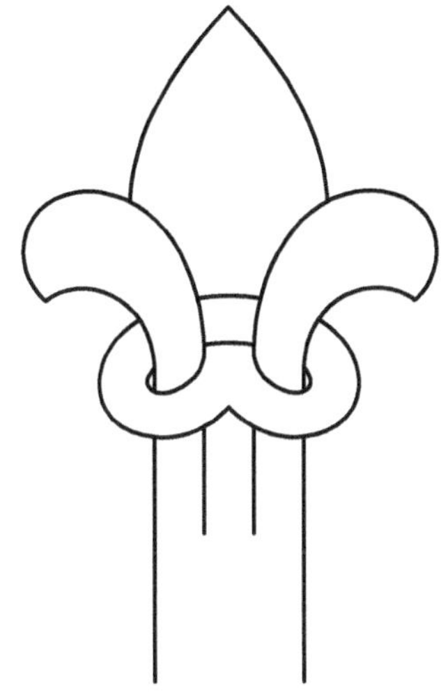

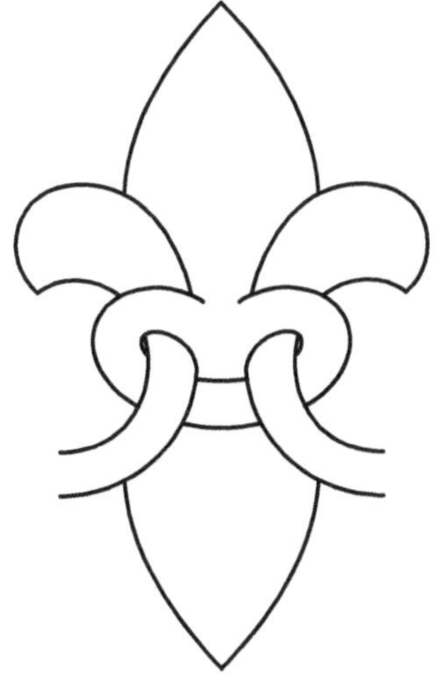

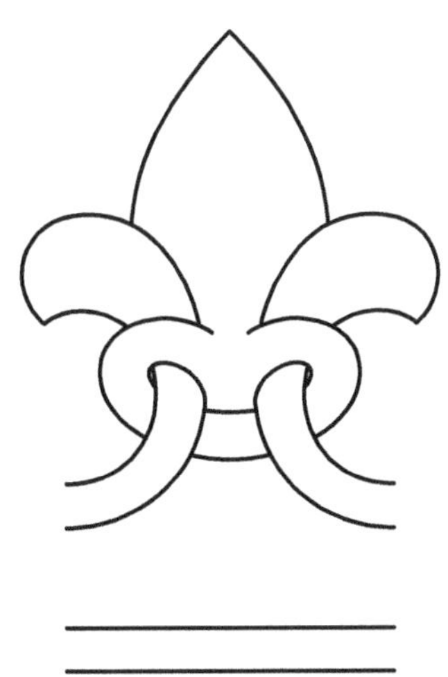

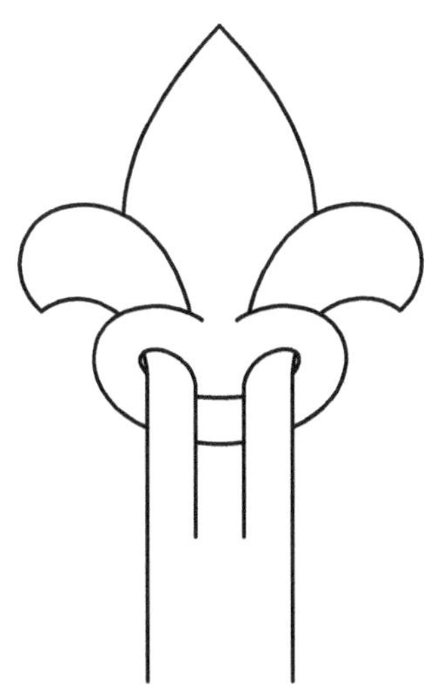

Top and Bottom Centre Lobes
A bottom centre lobe can be added, mirroring the top centre lobe.

Part of a Contour
The knot is placed at the edge of an element breaking the contour ribbon and wrapping it up into the knot to re-tie it.

Terminal Knot
The adjacent strands of the side lobes go straight down into a ribbon, making the union-knot motif a terminal piece of a ribbon.

Fleur-de-lis

Leaf Shapes

The fleur-de-lis motif comprises a centre lobe with a lobe at each side.

Rounded
The lobes can be rounded and curvy.

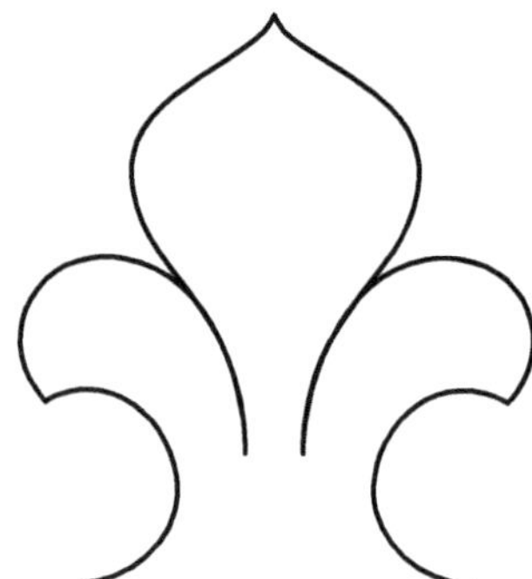

Rounded and Sharp
The lobes can be curvy and squat with pointy tips.

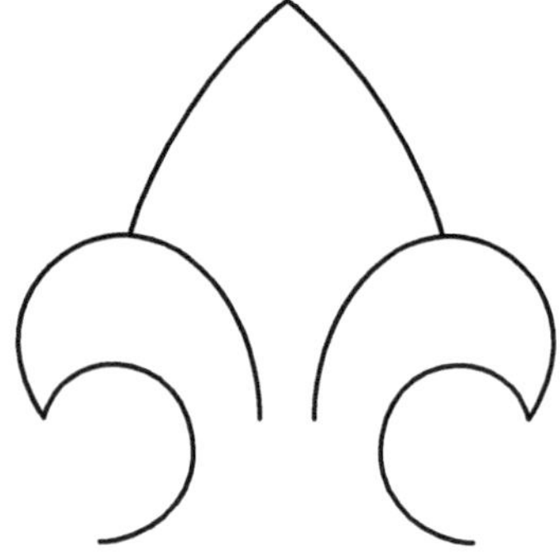

Sharp
The lobes can also be sharp and pointy.

Tendrils
One or more tendrils shooting off from in between the lobes occur, creating a more palmette-like motif.

Leaves
The side lobes can take the shape of fully-fledged acanthus leaves.

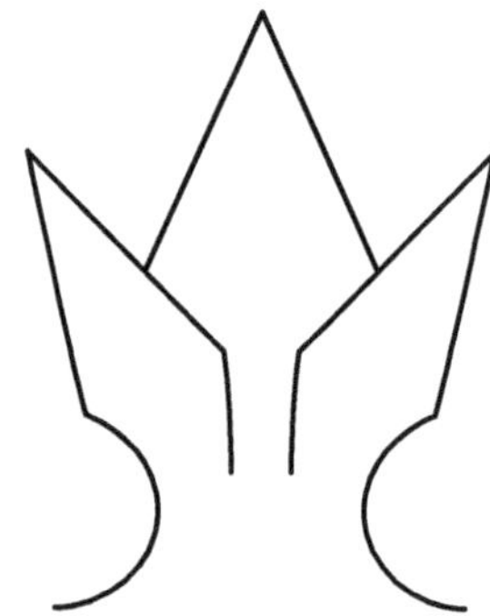

Diamonds
Some versions even have diamond-shaped lobes.

Fetters

The fleur-de-lis's lobes are often fettered together by a ring or knot.

Ring
The three lobes are often held together by a simple ring.

Upward-facing Union Knot
The lobes can also be held together by an upward-facing union knot.

Union Knot with Dented Loops
The loops of the union knot can have dents.

Ring with Petals
Sometimes the ring has a petal-like lobe-shaped silhouette.

Downward-facing Union Knot
Downward-facing union knots also occur.

Union Knot with Offshoots
The loops of the union knot can sprout tendrils, turning the fleur-de-lis into a palmette motif.

Feathering

Feathering a Ribbon

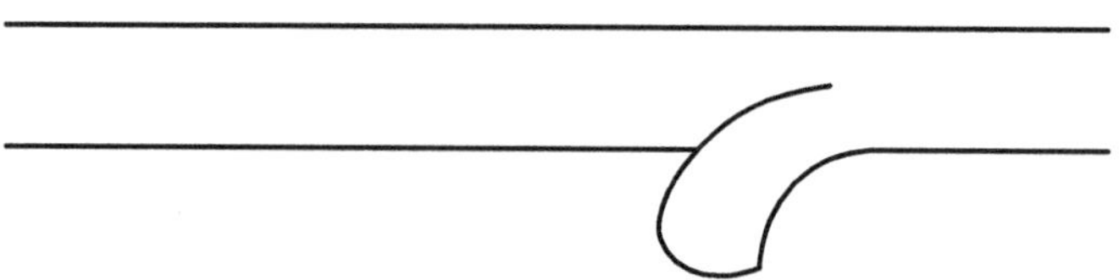

Adding a Single Lobe
A simple offshoot from a ribbon created by a single lobe peeling off from the edge of the ribbon, resembling a bud on a branch.

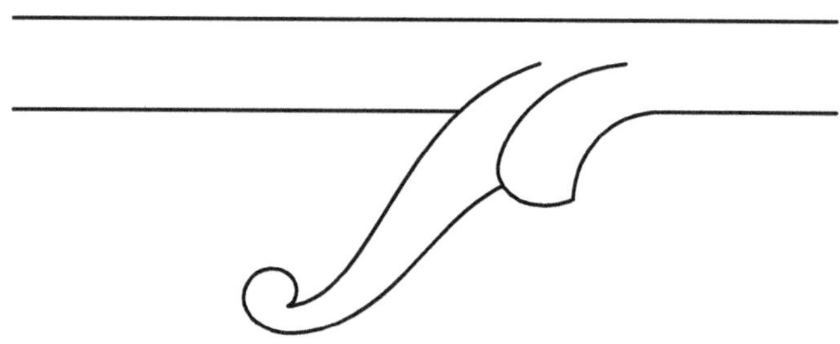

Adding the First Leaflet
Adding a leaflet in front of the lobe composes an acanthus leaf peeling off from the ribbon.

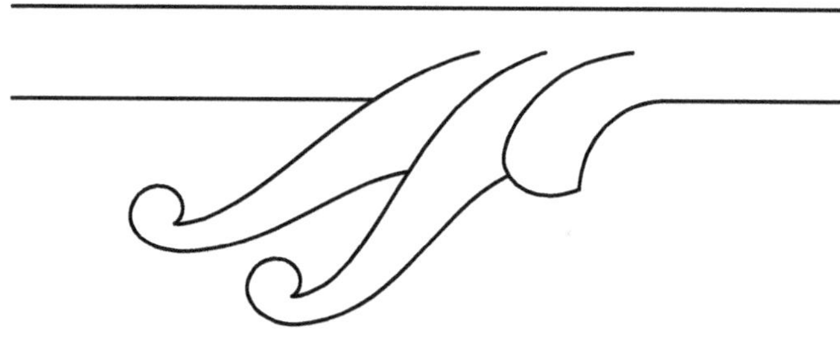

Adding Multiple Leaflets
Multiple additional leaflets can be added consecutively in front of the lobe.

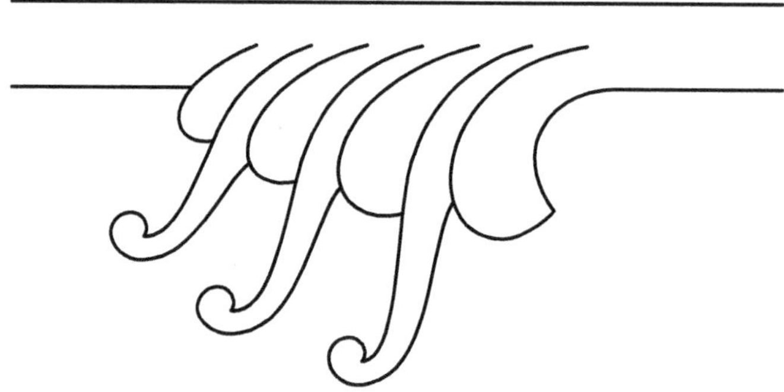

Expanding the Feather Structure
Adding additional strands alternating between lobes and leaflets create a feather-like structure.

Feathering a Leaf

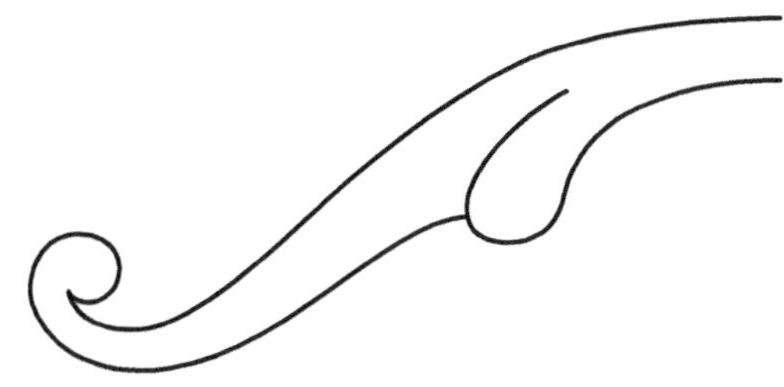

A Regular Leaf
A single acanthus-leaf motif comprises a leaflet with a lobe peeling off it.

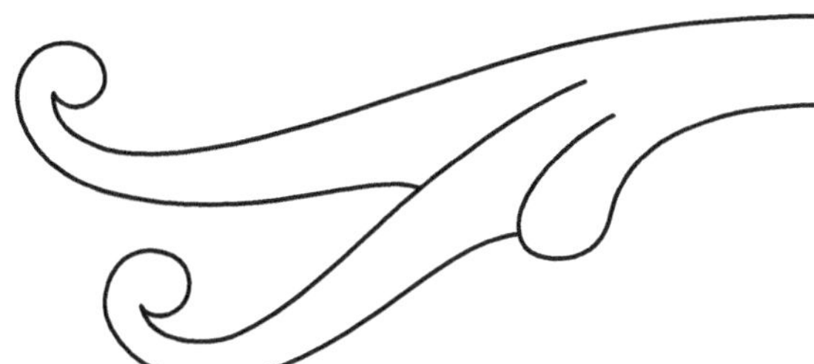

Adding Multiple Leaflets
One or more leaflets can be added on top of the first leaflet, similarly to the feathering of a ribbon.

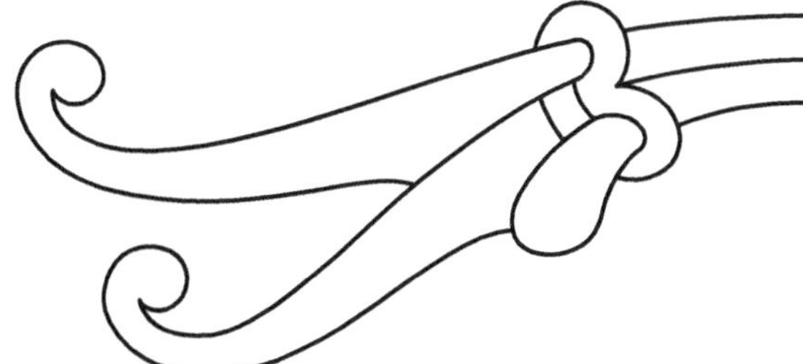

Adding a Union Knot
The middle leaflet is turned into a union knot, with its loops curling around the top leaflet and the lobe.

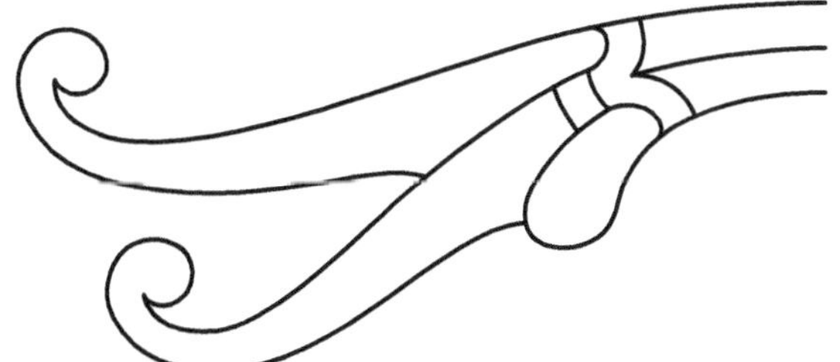

Cropping the Union Knot
The shape of the union knot is often simplified by shaving off the protruding loops at each side of the leaf, and the knot is also typically used in an even more trimmed-down version, as we'll see next.

Simple Fanning

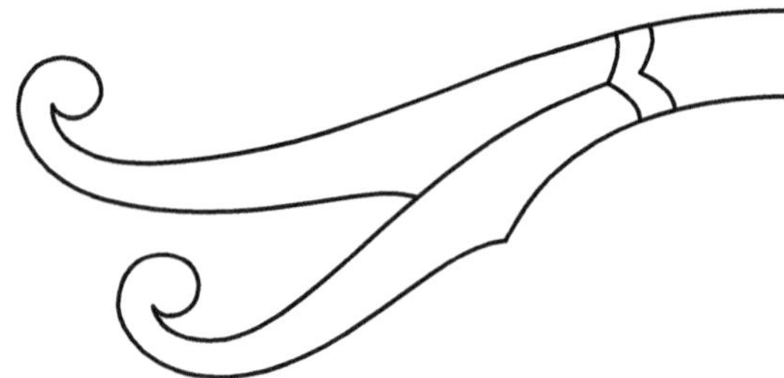

Two Leaflets Tied Together

A trimmed-down and simplified union-knot shape turned into a V-shaped ribbon snippet is often used to convey the splitting of a ribbon into two tendrils or leaflets.

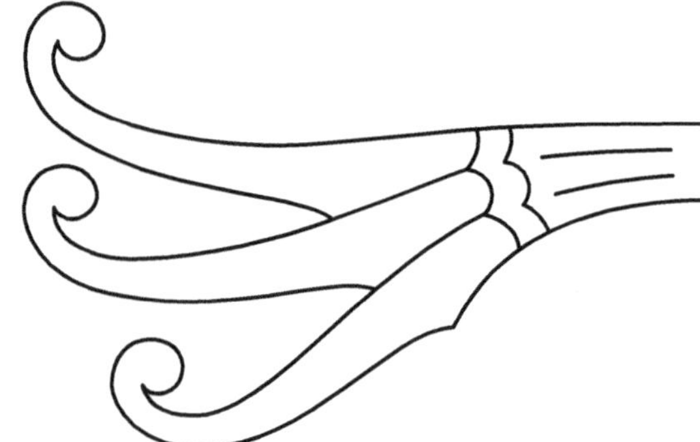

Three Leaflets Tied Together

Several V-shaped snippets can be combined to create a transverse wavy ribbon conveying multiple tendrils fanning out from the main ribbon.

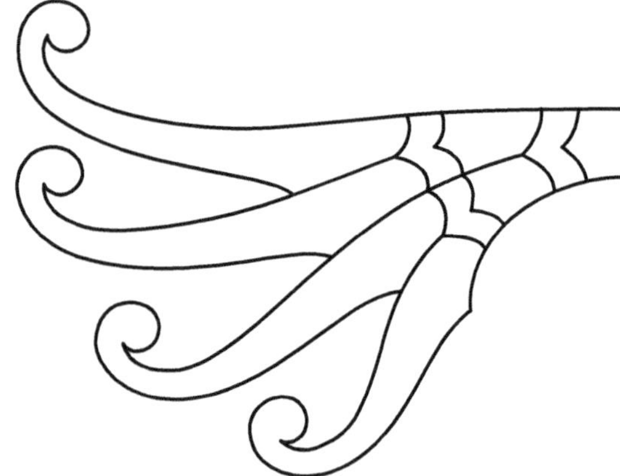

Four Leaflets with Double Tie

V-snippets can also be implemented on multiple levels of a tree-like bifurcating ribbon structure to create an extended fan motif.

Elaborate Fanning

Wing

A feathered wing motif can be created by fanning leaflets alternating between tendril and lobe shapes.

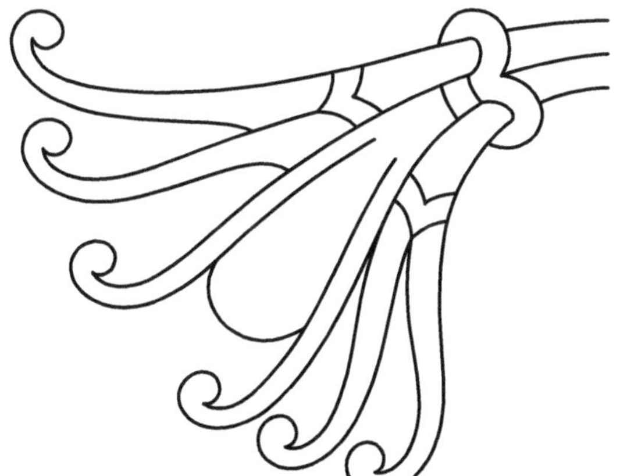

Tailpiece

An elaborate dovetail can be created with a union knot in the centre surrounded by fanning leaflets at each side.

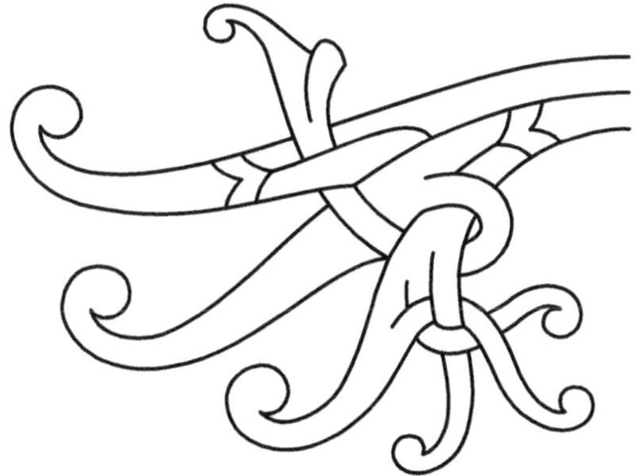

Headpiece

The intricate headpieces of the beasts are usually created by combining several loops and knots with fanning tendril leaflets to create a multi-layered knotwork pattern shooting off from the head.

Palmette from Union Knot

Simple

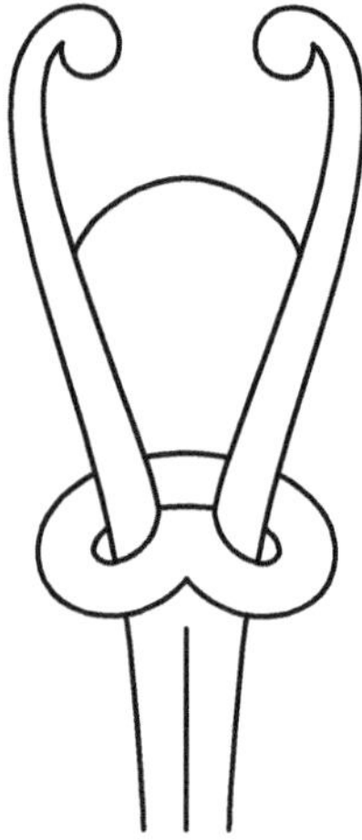

Core Structure
A palmette can be created from a union knot motif terminating a ribbon. Two strands extend upwards from the ribbon stem splitting in two and forking off to each side. The two strands are joined by a union knot terminating in a centre lobe.

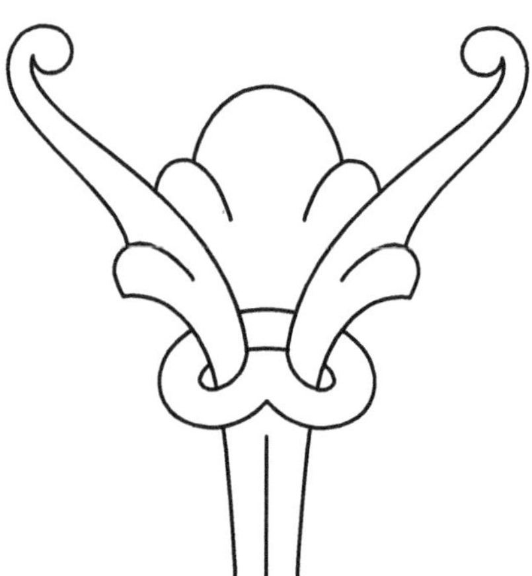

Splitting the Lobe and Leaflets
The simplest way to expand the core palmette is to turn the centre lobe into a fleur-de-lis and the side strands into acanthus leaves by adding lobes.

Split Centre Strand

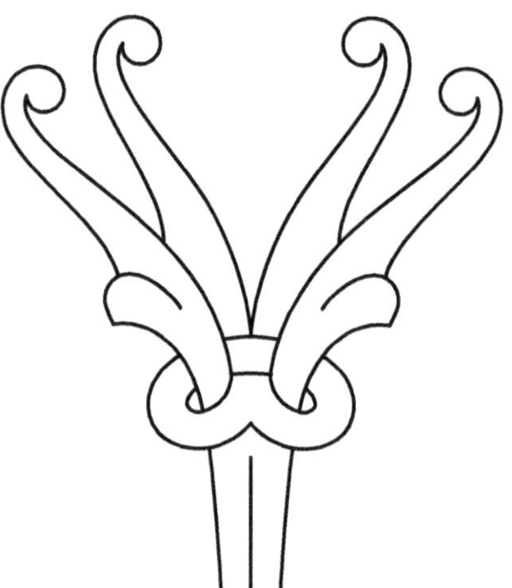

Turning the Centre-lobe into Leaflets
The centre lobe can be split into two or more leaflets.

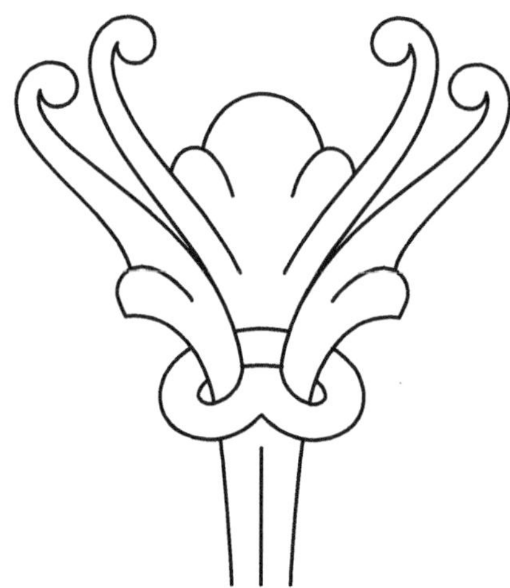

Fleur-de-lis with Leaflets
Leaflets can also be added in between the side leaves and the centre lobe to create additional levels of foliage.

Split Side Strands

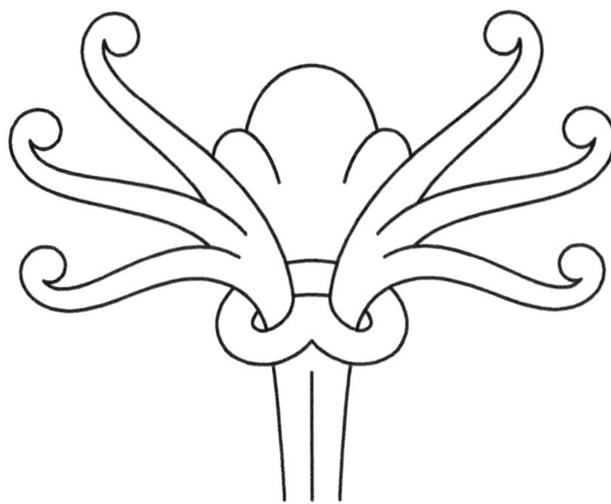

Fanning Out the Side Strands
Another way to expand the palmette is to split the two leaflets at the sides into branches fanning out into multiple strands of leaflets.

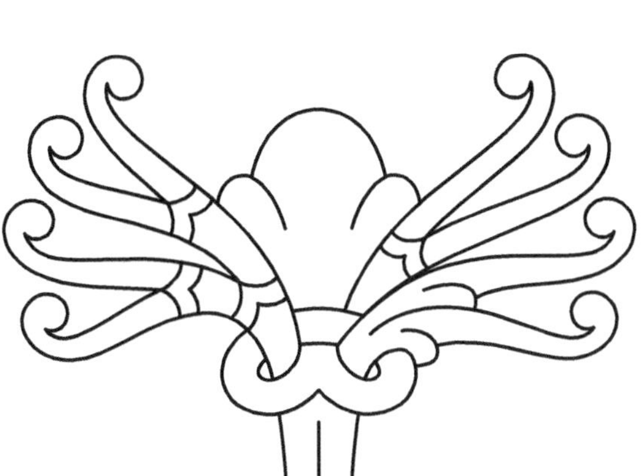

Add Variation to the Side-branches
Additional branches can be added between the centre lobe and the side branches. Reconfiguring the strands into asymmetrical multi-layered fanning structures creates variation.

Elaborate

Offshoots from the Union Knot
Add acanthus-leaf offshoots to the two loops of the knot to create an extra level of foliage.

Further Reconfigurations
Reconfigure additional elements like flipping the union knot upside-down and turning the centre lobe into the shape of a braided loop with interlocking tendrils to create a customised design.

Palmette from Ribbon

Single Loop

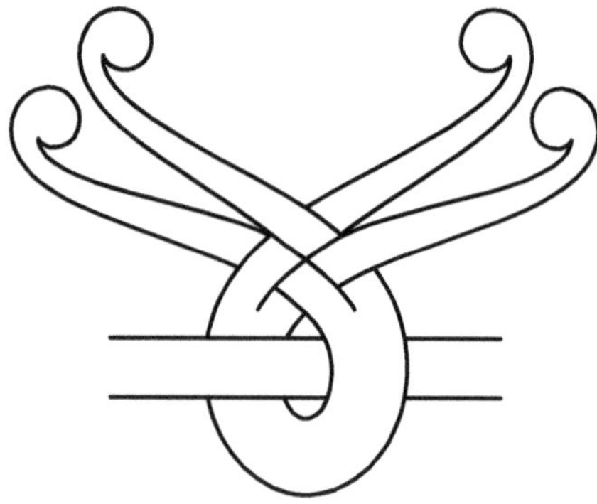

Loop with Braided Tendrils
A basic palmette can be created by a simple looping ribbon with interlocking tendrils curling around a stem.

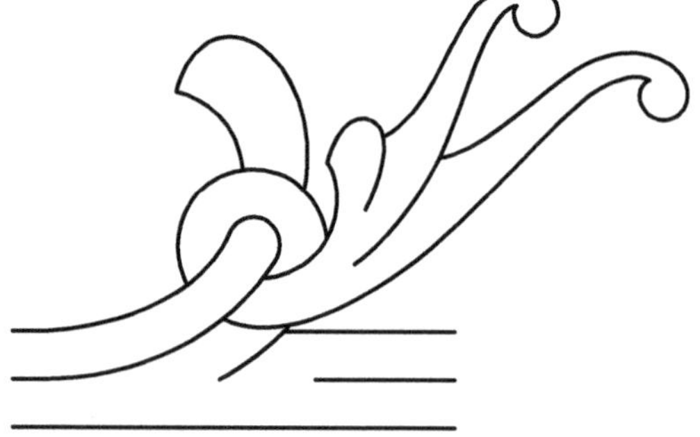

Looping Offshoot
Two parallel tendrils shooting off from a stem, the inner tendril looping around the outer tendril creates the base structure of a palmette offshoot.

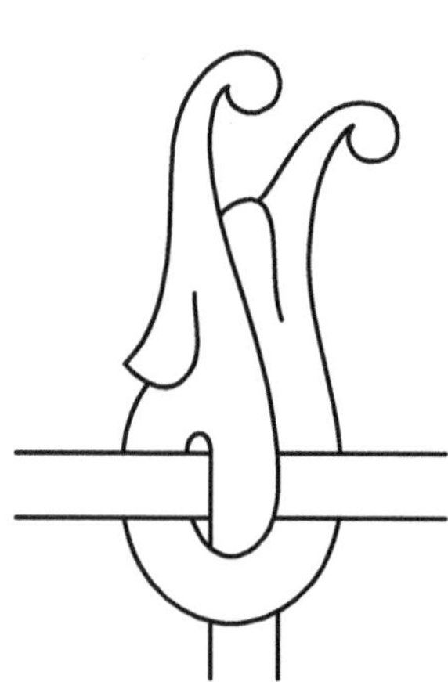

Tied Loop with Parallel Leaves
Another simple way is to tie a ribbon around a stem. Add an acanthus leaf offshoot to the curve of the loop and make the leaf terminal of the ribbon align parallel to it.

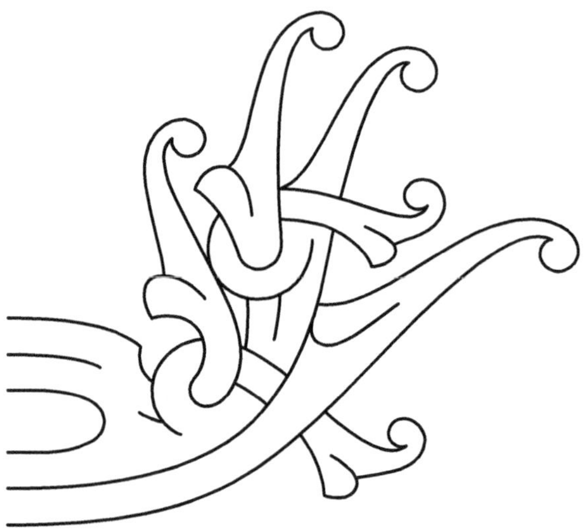

Curve with Multiple Offshoots
Multiple levels of looping offshoots sitting at the outer edge of a curling ribbon.

Pretzel Knot

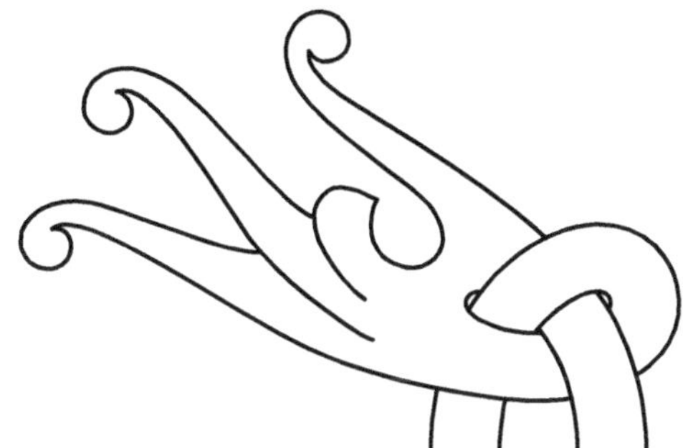

Pretzel Knot Loop
The loop of a pretzel knot is an excellent base for a palmette.

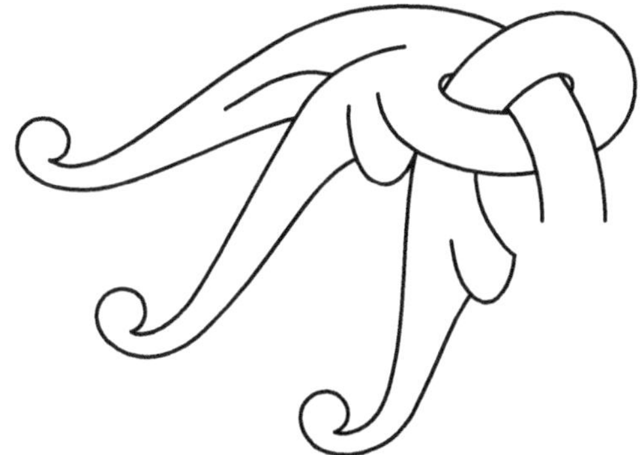

Pretzel-knot Loop and Ribbon End
The end of the ribbon can be incorporated into the pretzel palmette to add an additional layer.

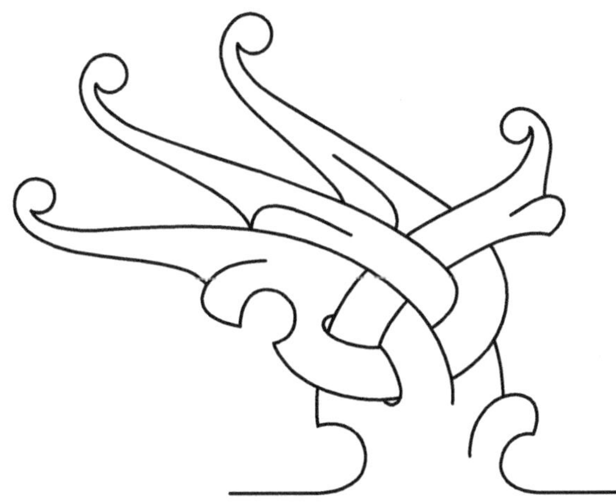

Pretzel-knot Offshoot
The pretzel-knot can also be connected to the edge of a ribbon or figure to create a multilayered pretzel-offshoot palmette.

Beast Head Variations

The appearance of beast heads can be exceptionally varied while still sticking to the core structural principles.

Minimal Features

- The most minimalist rendering is composed of a simple and streamlined outline of the head.
- The only other features needed for a complete and recognisable head are the eye and the teeth.

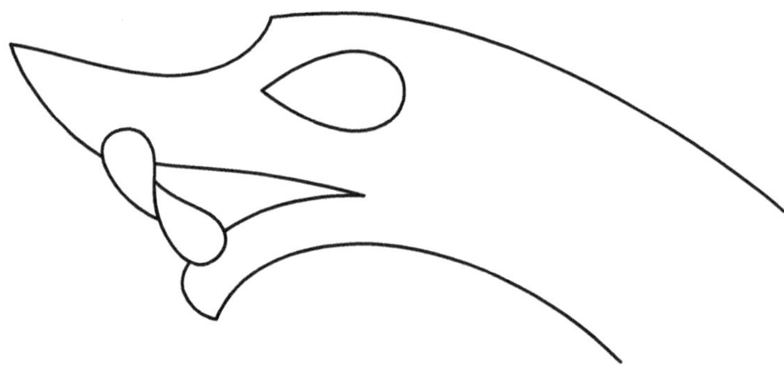

Simple Features

- The lip lappet is a typical and prevalent feature.
- Two triangular shapes on top of the head will give the animal a wolf-like appearance.
- S-shaped locks of hair along the neck compose a common mane-like feature.

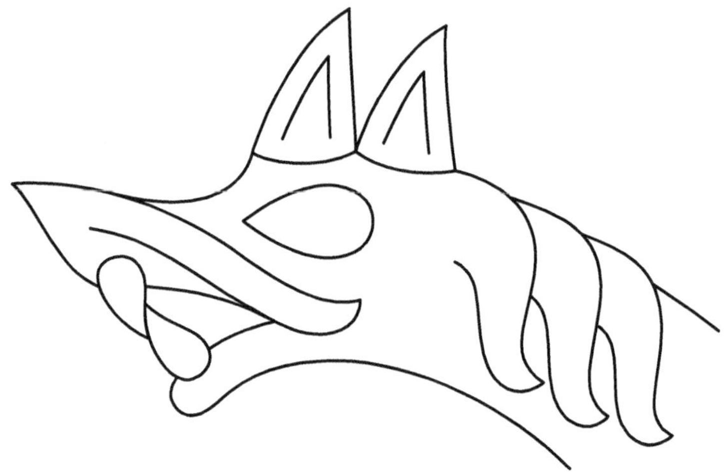

Classic Features

- A lip lappet with its tip curled up in a spiral-ball terminal is an iconic feature.
- The locks of the mane are curled up into spiral-ball terminals as well.
- The ears are often turned into a symmetric crest in the shape of a fleur-de-lis motif.
- Two lobes on each side of the top tooth are common.
- An S-shaped tongue with a spiral-ball terminal rolls out the mouth.

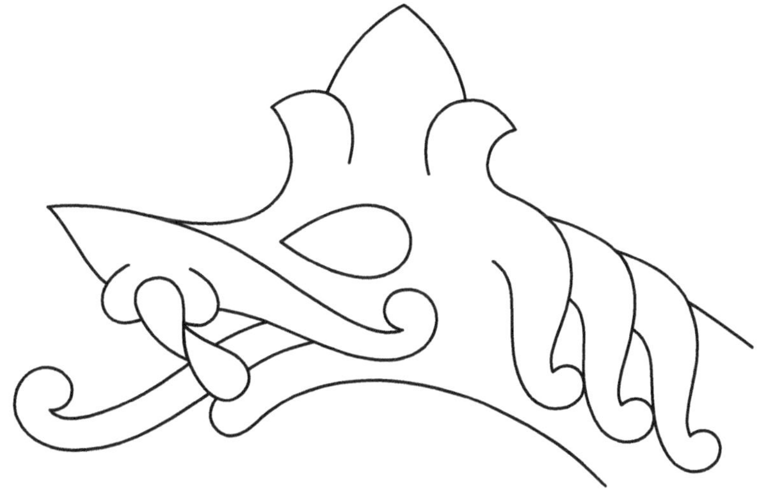

Elaborate Features

- A ribbon snippet sits above the top tooth, splitting the snout in two between its tip and the lip lappet.
- Adding a lobe to the lip lappet turns it into an acanthus leaf.
- The crest is turned into an intricate asymmetric knotwork piece iconic for the style.
- A spiral sits at the top of the neck as a base for the mane.
- Lobes are added to the locks of the mane to turn them into acanthus leaves.
- An S-shaped ribbon curls along the top of the eye and down towards the neck to create an eyebrow.

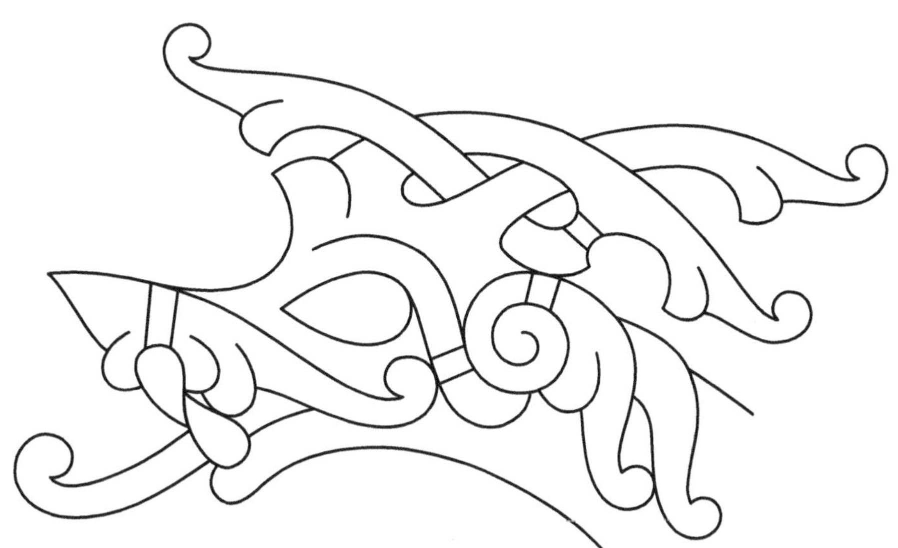

Beast Feet Variations

There is surprisingly slight variation in the rendition of feet in Ringerike style proper.

The most significant variation is a product of stylistic evolution from the late Mammen style, through Ringerike, to the early Urnes style.

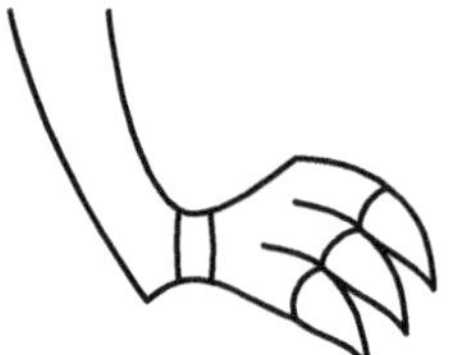

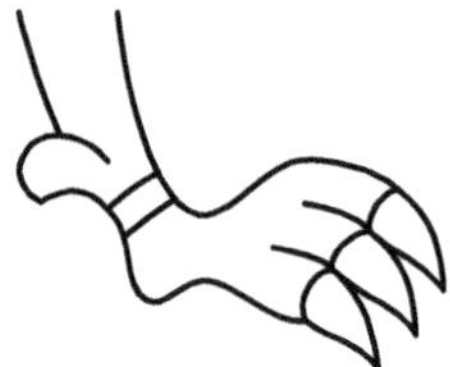

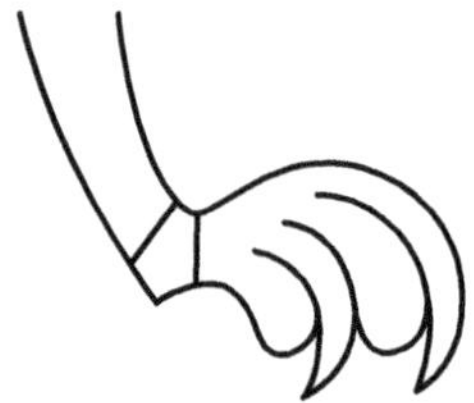

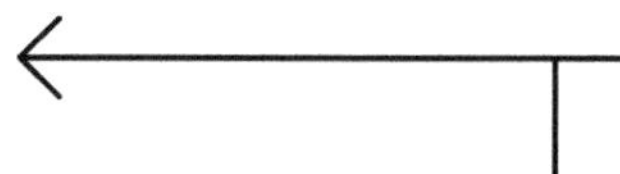

Early Ringerike Style

- An overall squat and curvy, almost naturalistic paw-like shape.
- Usually featuring three toes.
- Defined triangular claws.
- A transverse ribbon snippet across the ankle joint or the arch occurs.
- Occasionally, a backwards-facing lobe.

More elaborate variations can be created by applying some of the typical ornamental motifs and mechanics of the Ringerike style (exemplified by the paw with the feathered claws right above).

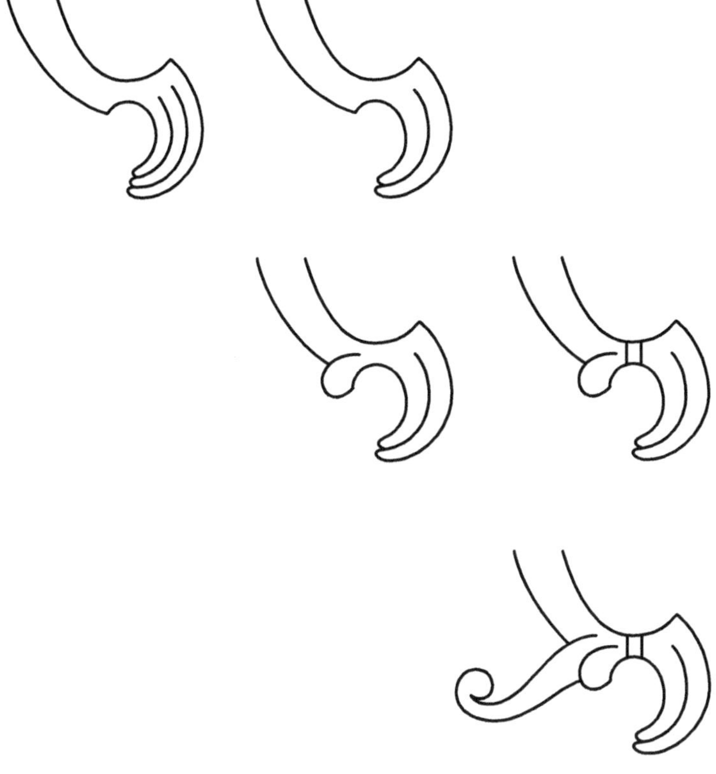

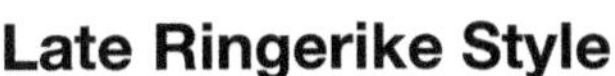

Ringerike Style Proper

- An overall slender, almost crescent moon-like shape, with sharp corners at the knuckles and the heel.
- Two or three toes without articulated claws.
- Occasionally, a backwards-facing lobe.
- A transverse ribbon snippet across the ankle joint occurs.

The backwards-facing lobe can be more or less elaborate, for instance, functioning as a base for tendril offshoots or being extended into a full acanthus leaf.

Late Ringerike Style

- Overall, simpler and more uniform, the shape of the feet tends to trend towards the S-shaped sway typical for the Urnes style.
- Two or three toes.
- The backwards-facing lobe is a standard feature.

The Design Process

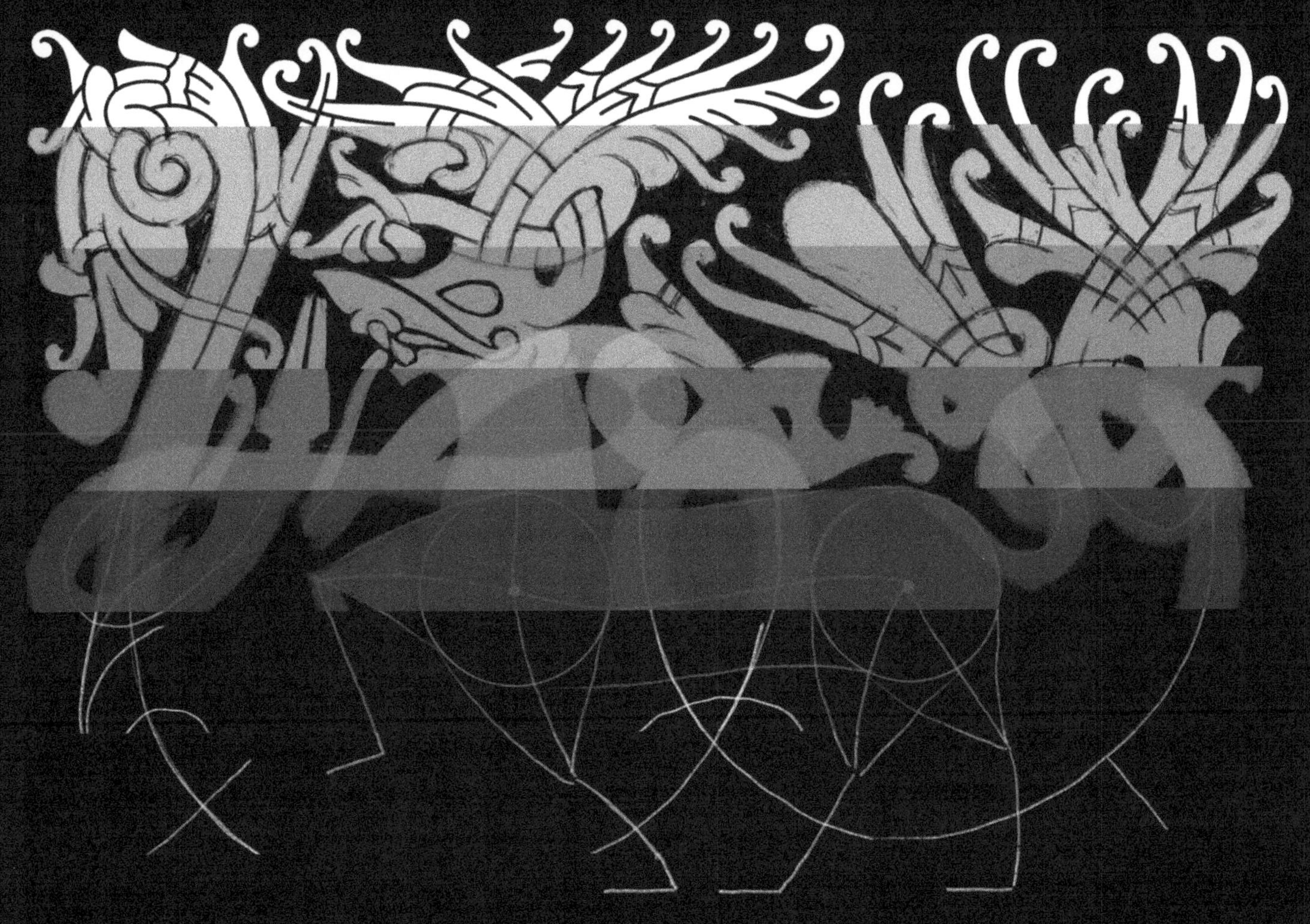

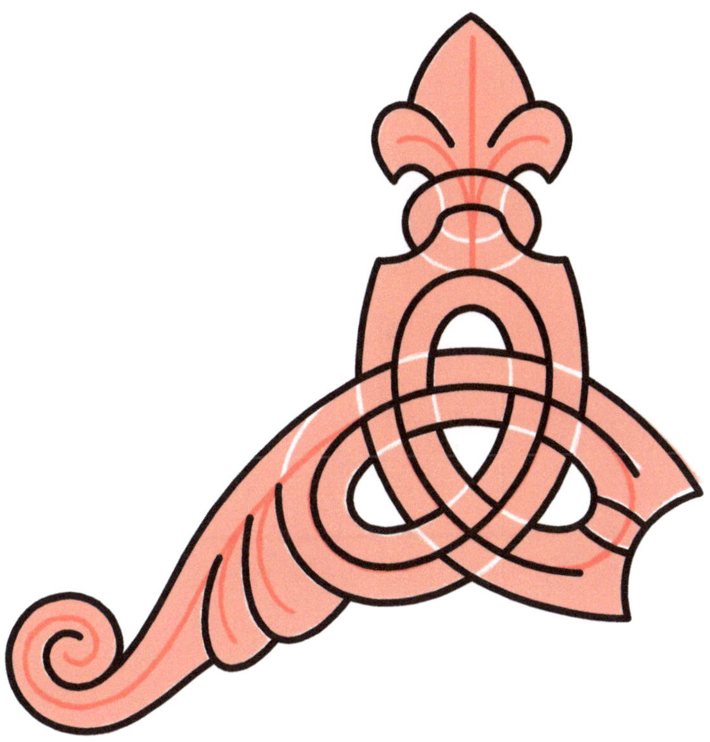

Sampling from the Historical Designs

We'll look at the trends and characteristics of historical designs of great beast motifs. Researching the composition and features of original designs is an essential source of inspiration for your new design.

Then we'll look at your new design's components based on the Ringerike style principles. You'll see how the historical elements are incorporated directly into the new design.

This will give you a thorough understanding of the concrete components composing the great beast composition you're about to create.

Analysing the References

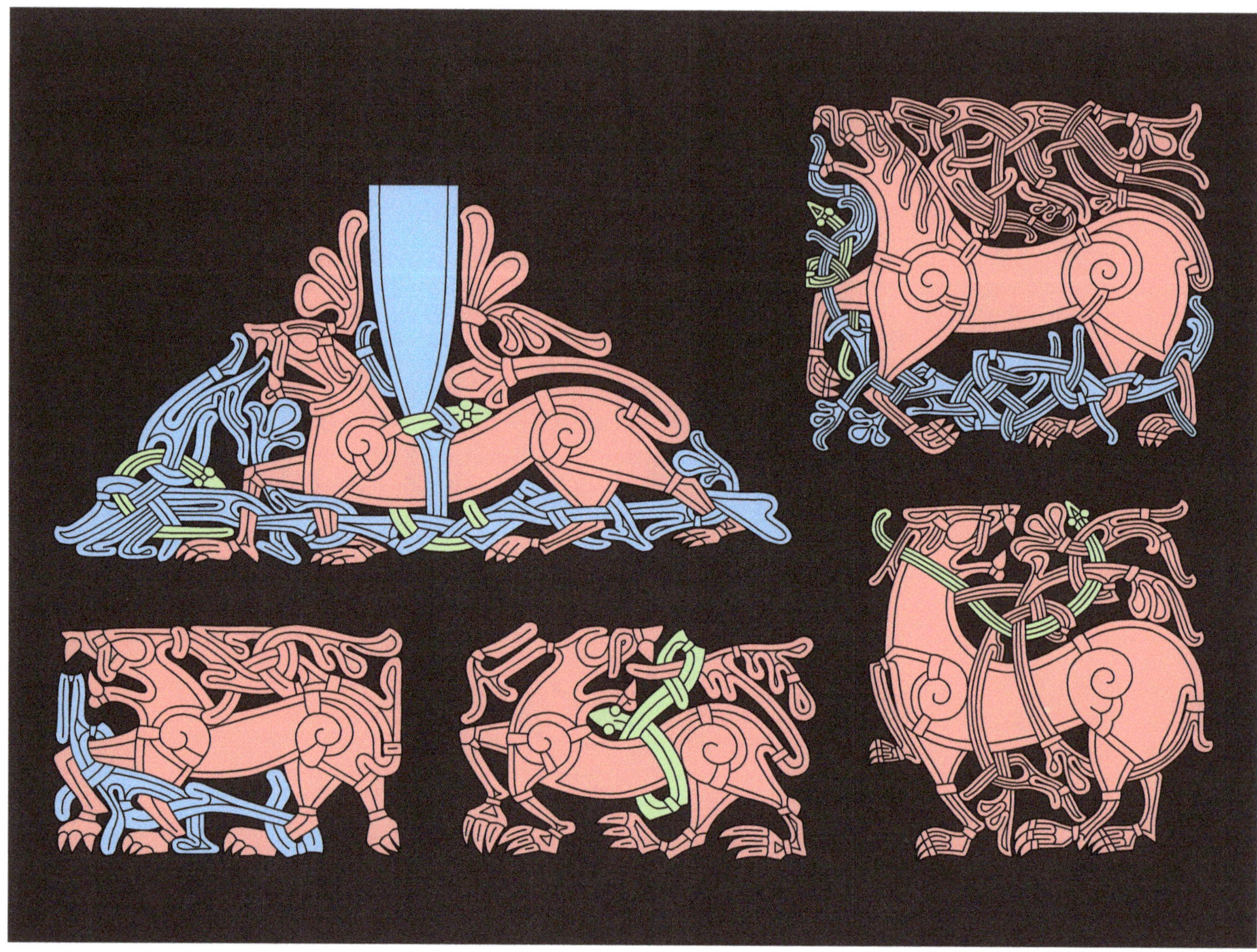

Composition

Comparing a selection of the historical designs, some common trends and individual differences appear.

Please Note
- The designs on the left page trend towards early Ringerike and late Mammen style. But they still contain many useful standard Ringerike style characteristics.
- Some of the designs shown above have been mirrored for easy comparison.

Compositional Elements
- Beasts
- Vines
- Serpents

Beasts

Some beasts have crossed legs, while most have spread legs as if the animal is moving forward. The left-side feet are usually positioned behind the right-side feet.

The legs are often tied by interlacing vines or serpents as if to immobilise the beast.

The crest of the beast's head is sometimes articulated in a simple and short crown-like manner by a few lobes or leaves. Still, it can also

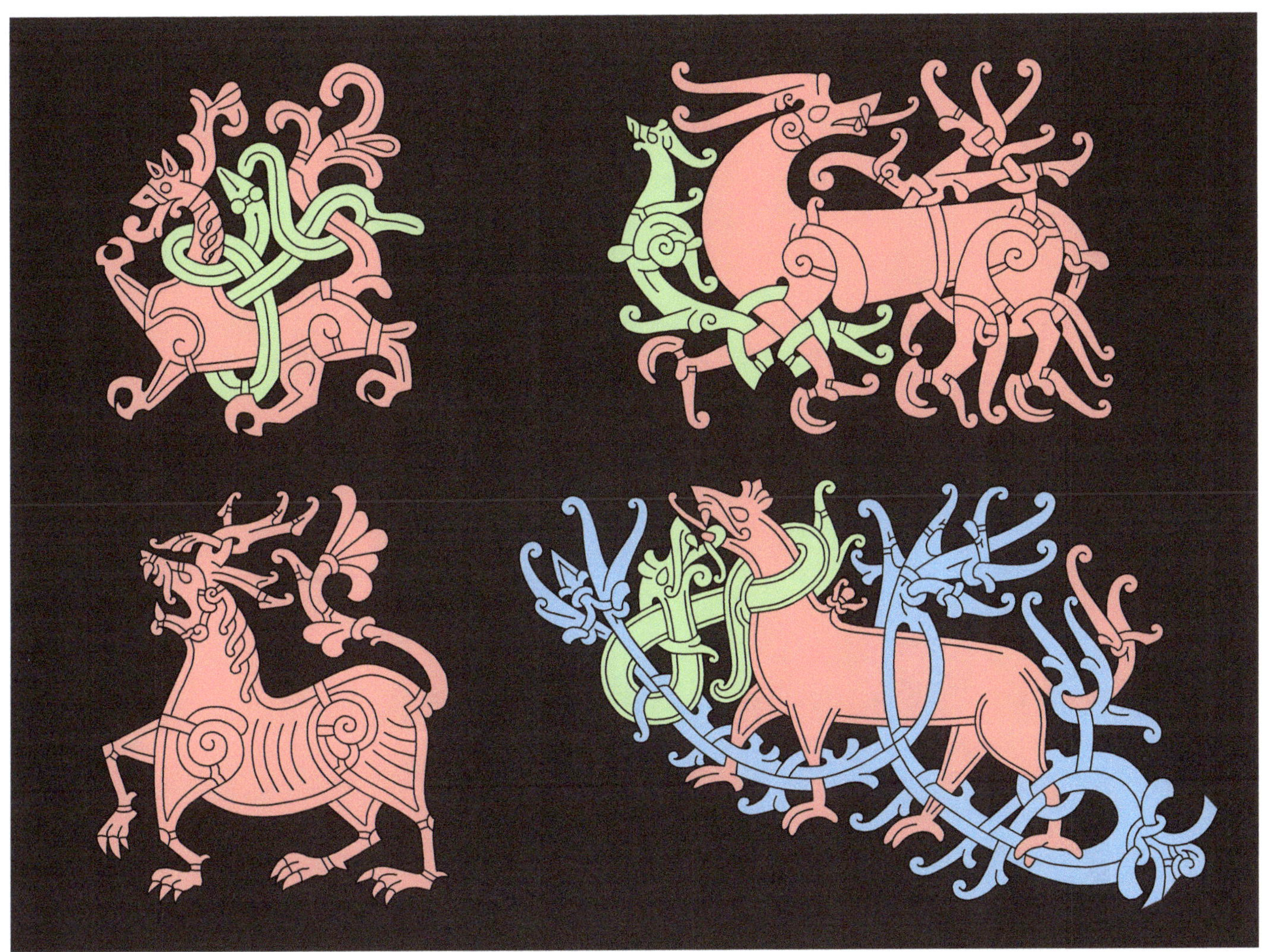

compose an extensive, elaborate neck tendril interlacing with the surrounding knotwork pattern.

The beast's tail usually interlaces with the knotwork pattern, either above or below the beast's body. The terminal of the tail can virtually take any shape within the confines of Ringerike-style principles.

Serpents and Vines

Although the designs may look very similar at first glance, and the overall theme seems to be a beast caught in interlacing ribbons, they vary significantly in detail at a closer look.

Often a common denominator is a ribbon looping around the beast's stomach, sometimes tying the legs with smaller loops. But how the ribbons flow and lock the limbs varies.

Usually, the beast is wrapped by one or more serpents. But not always, sometimes it's a vine fettering the beast, and sometimes it's both.

Serpents are often very simple in shape, but more elaborate variations occur.

The variation in the vines is significant. They easily fill in vacant background space when necessary with elaborate offshoots and palmettes.

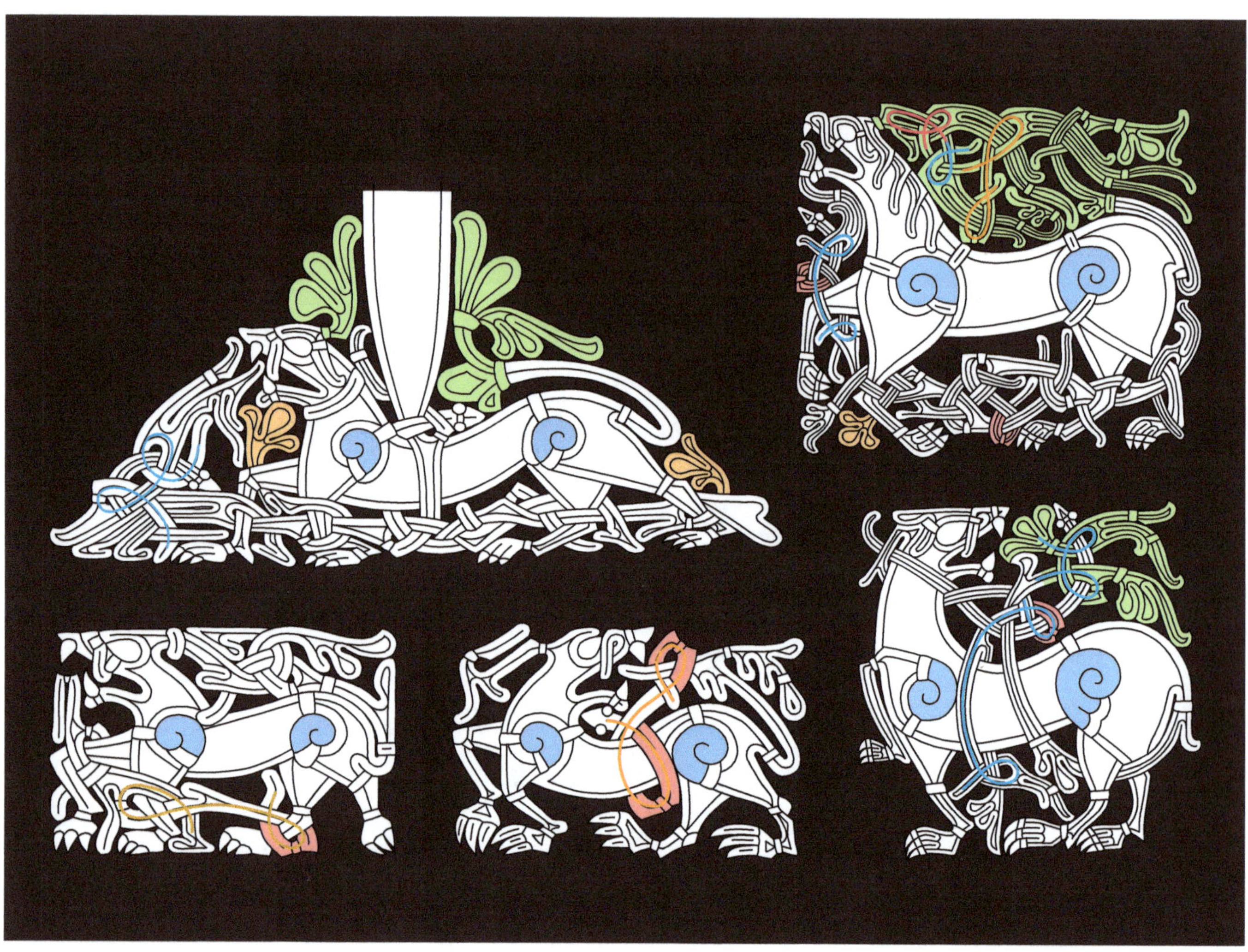

Details

As with the details of the configuration of the compositions, there's generally also fairly significant variation in the application of loops, knots and ornamental motifs, but some general principles and trends can be gleaned from the historical designs.

Loops and Knots
— Figure-eights
— Curly loops
— Pretzel knots
— Union knots

Ornamental Motifs
● Spirals
● Palmettes
● Dented loops
● Fleur-de-lis

Loops and Knots

Figure-eights
Serpents are usually curling in figure-eights, but not exclusively, and figure-eights are generally used sparingly in the context of great beast compositions.

Curly Loops
The ribbon curling around the beast's stomach is often a curly loop. Vines are usually curled in curly loops, but not exclusively. Other ribbon elements also use this looping scheme, which is the most prevalent in the Ringerike style.

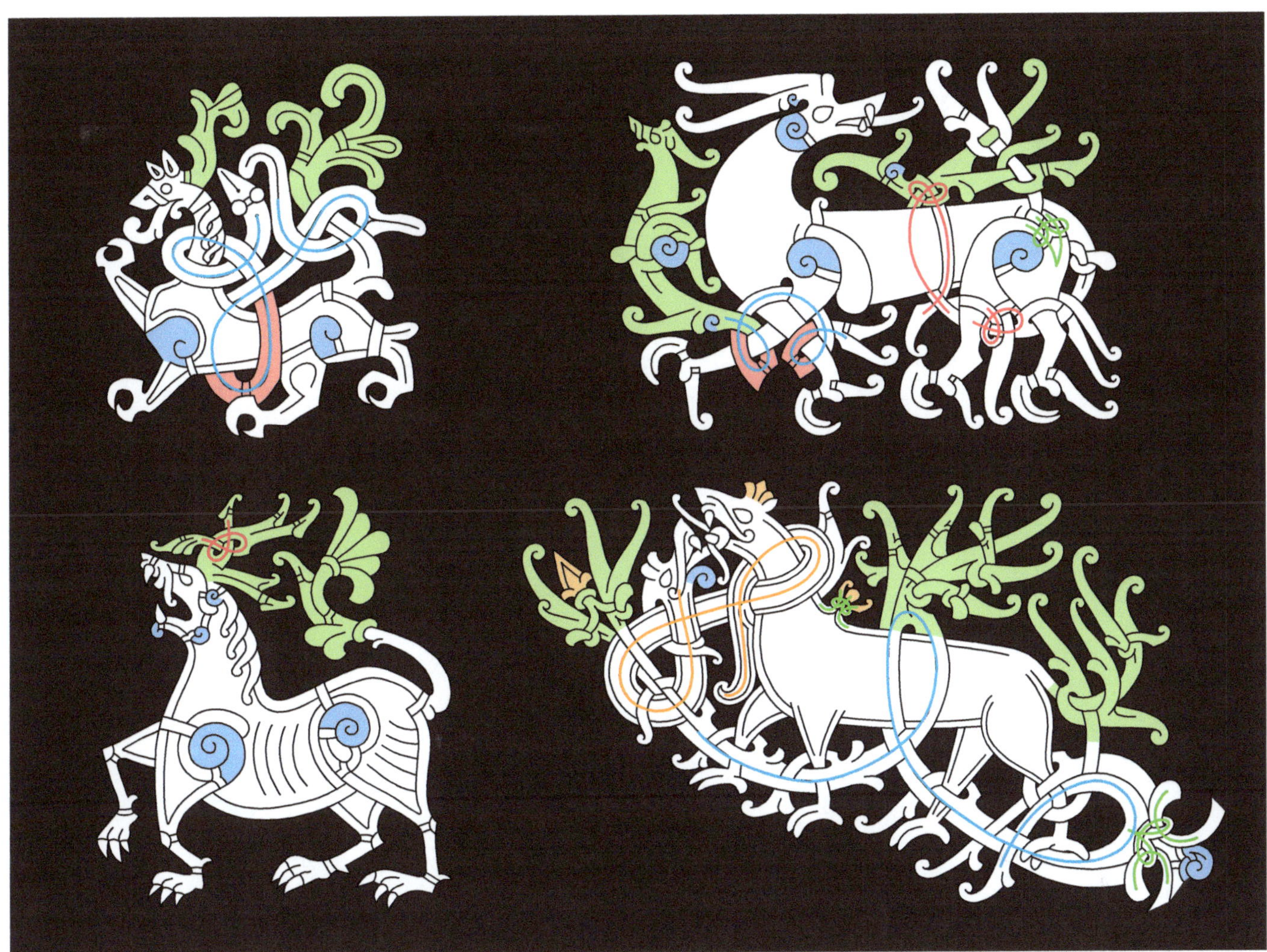

Pretzel Knots

In great beast compositions, pretzel knots are primarily used for tertiary ribbons to create bases for multiple offshoots.

Union Knots

Union knots are used selectively and creatively to customise the look of the designs whenever they occur.

Ornamental Motifs

Spirals

Most beasts, but not all, have spiral hips. And some smaller spirals also occur in other places, like the lip of the bottom jaw and the neck of some animals, as well as part of the bases for ornamental offshoots.

Palmettes

Most palmettes are in the shape of the beast's neck tendril or tail. Though palmettes sprouting from vines occur too

Dented Loops

Dented loops are common in the loops of the serpent ribbon bodies.

Fleur-de-lis

The fleur-de-lis motif is used selectively as an extra flourish when appropriate but is not necessary.

Breaking Down the Composition

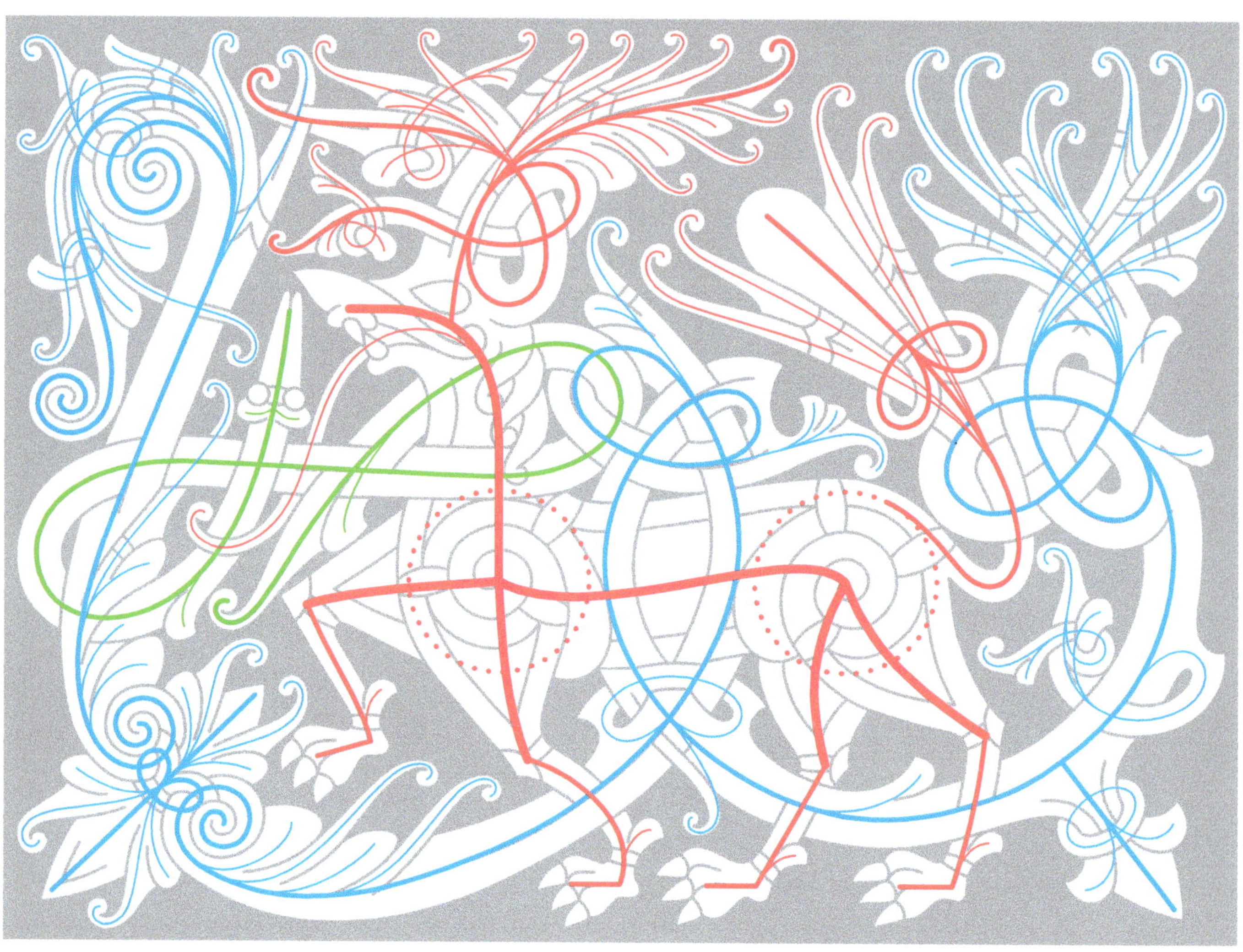

Composition and Details

The new design is created based on the Ringerike style principles by sampling from the historical references.

Primary, secondary and tertiary ribbons construct the hierarchically tiered ribbon bodies and vines.

The compositional elements of the beast, vine and serpent interlock and fill out the background with knotwork patterns and strategically placed palmettes.

Ribbons
— Beast
— Vine
— Serpent

Shapes
● Beast
● Vine
● Serpent

Beast

The beast composes the primary ribbon as the main compositional focus. The animal is oriented to the left, with its head facing forward. The legs are spread, and the right front leg is raised and bent.

The beast's tail and crest compose ribbons weaving with the ribbon branches of the vine.

The beast's tail terminates in a palmette tied in a union knot. The crest has a pretzel knot at its base, sprouting a multilayered palmette of acanthus leaves, one of the leaves with feathering.

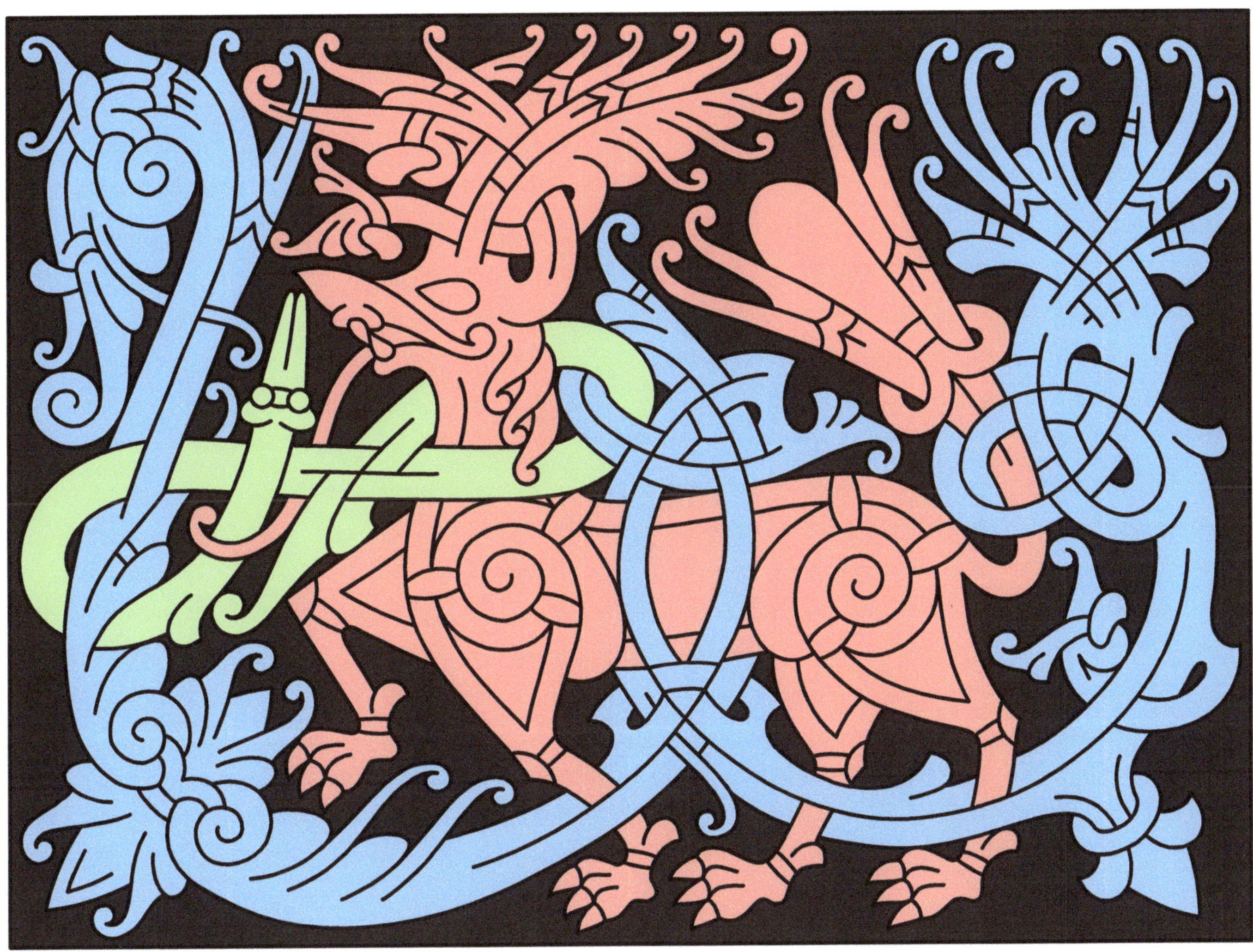

Vine

The vine wraps around the beast in a curly loop, with its ends filling out the vacant background.

The vine's base is rooted in the bottom left corner in two spirals connected by a union knot. From each spiral sprouts a double-stranded ribbon stem with feathering at the bases.

One stem grows vertically upwards, unfurling in a spiral palmette in the top left corner.

The other stem grows horisontally to the right, wraps around the beast's body in a double knot, and travels between the legs curling upwards behind the beast, sprouting a fleur-de-lis in the bottom right corner to mirror the base of the vine, and a tendril loop along the way. The stem terminates in a triquetra knot, wrapping around the beast's tail with a braided palmette sprouting from the triquetra's top loop.

Serpent

The serpent curls in a simple figure-eight, looping around the neck of the beast and the stem of the vine.

It is traditional and simple but has tight interlace locking its mid-section with its tail.

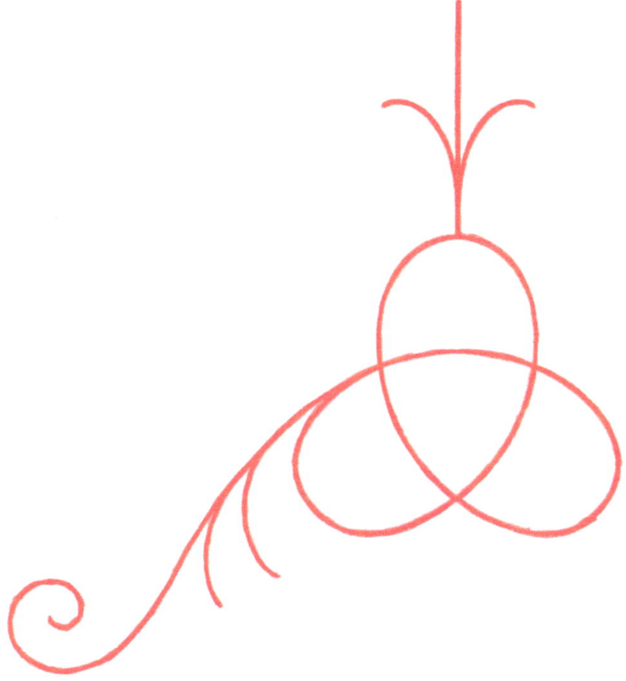

Main Compositional Lines and Ribbon Flow

This phase will create the structure and backbone for the rest of your design process.

To get going, you'll arrange the flow of the ribbons of the design. This will let you plan out the entire composition swiftly, encountering any knotwork issues that need fixing before you'll put a lot of work into the design.

First, you'll begin with the primary ribbon lines in the shape of the great beast comprising the centrepiece of the composition. Around the beast, you'll add the secondary lines in the shape of vines and a serpent. Lastly, you'll add the tertiary ribbons in the shape of knots and tendrils shooting off from and adding to the primary and secondary ribbons.

Tip: Work in Layers

You might want to work on a new layer stacked on top of the previous one for each step of the design process.

If you work digitally, you can add a new layer and adjust the opacity of the layer below. You might even want to assign separate layers for each main element, like the beast, vine and serpent.

If you work with pen and paper, you can use a lightbox and stack sheets of paper on top of each other. Or you can use a semitransparent medium like manifold paper if you don't have a lightbox.

Arranging the Primary Ribbons

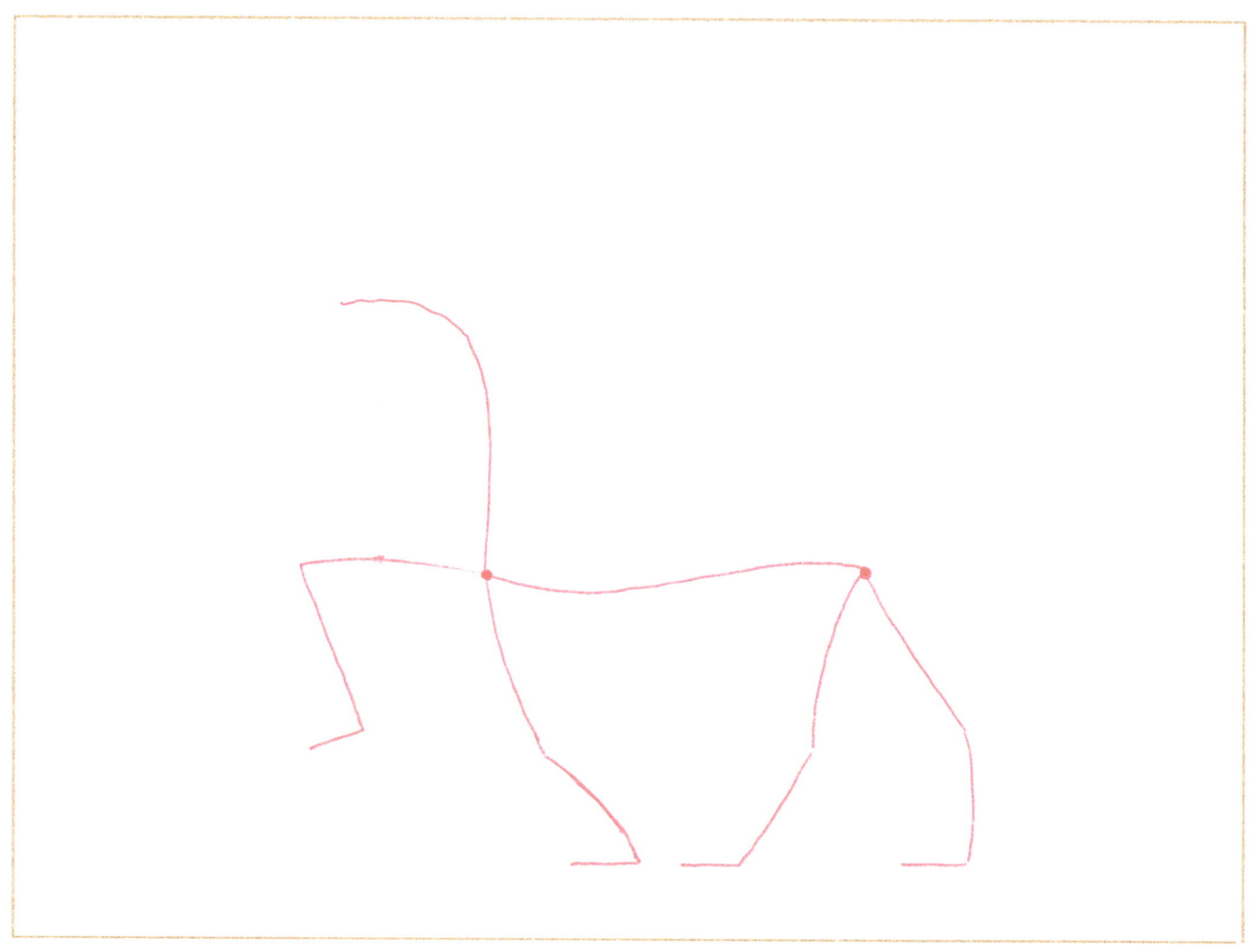

Choose your canvas

To begin the design, you need to decide on the size and proportions of the canvas.

You can let your medium of choice determine the size of your design and fit your composition into a pre-existing canvas. Or, you can choose a canvas size that fits the content of a design you already have in mind. Either way, the design will be modified to fit the canvas by making the knotwork pattern fill the vacant spaces around the central motif of the composition.

Beast: Ribbon Flow

The composition's primary ribbon and main lines will take the shape of a great beast composing the centrepiece.

Start the illustration by sketching the ribbon flow of the beast's main limbs: its body, four legs and neck.

Mark the centre of the two hips with two dots.

Connect the two hips by drawing the spinal ribbon line from dot to dot.

Add in the four legs hinging at the centre of the hips, each bending at the knee and ankle.

Draw the neckline up vertically from the centre of the front hip, curling forward into where the horizontally aligned head will be.

Model the stance of the animal and the direction of its head to your liking. The beast can, for example, look forward or backwards, raise its right front leg, or stand on all four legs.

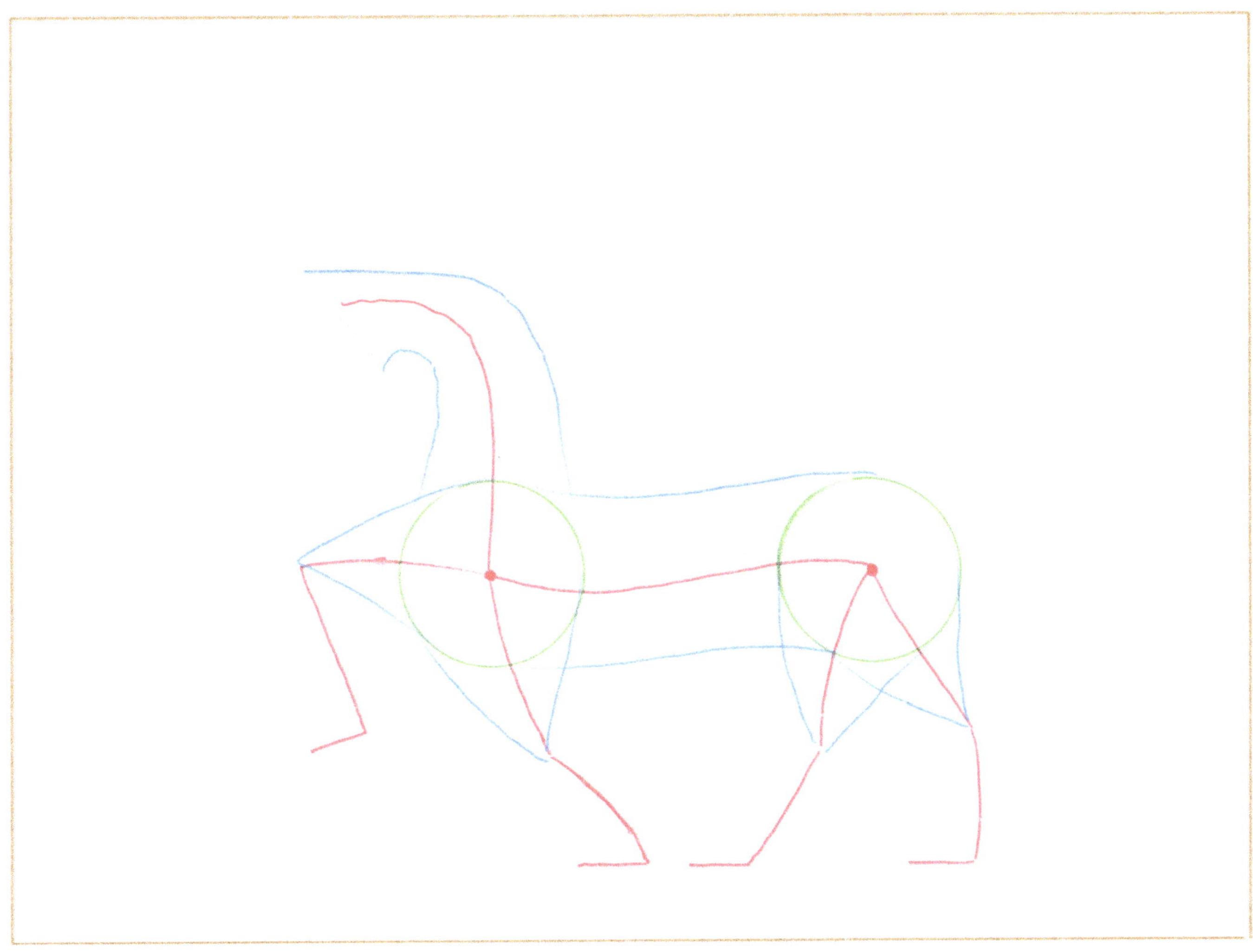

Beast: Rough Outline

Knowing how much space the beast's limbs take up is crucial to distribute the remaining ribbons evenly around it. To get a sense of the negative space around the animal, lightly sketch in the main outlines of the beast. We'll fill in the animal body more effectively later in the process, so a rough outline is more than enough for now.

Start by adding in the circumference of the hips around the hip centres. This will give you a base measure for the thickness of the animal body.

Add in the outlines of the back and stomach above and under the spine to mark the width of the beast's body.

Mark the thighs with four triangular shapes tapering in from the hip circles with the point of the triangles ending at the knees.

The neck tapers slightly, curling towards the head on both the front and back.

The top outline of the head goes horizontally, and the lower jawline curls downwards.

Arranging the Secondary Ribbons

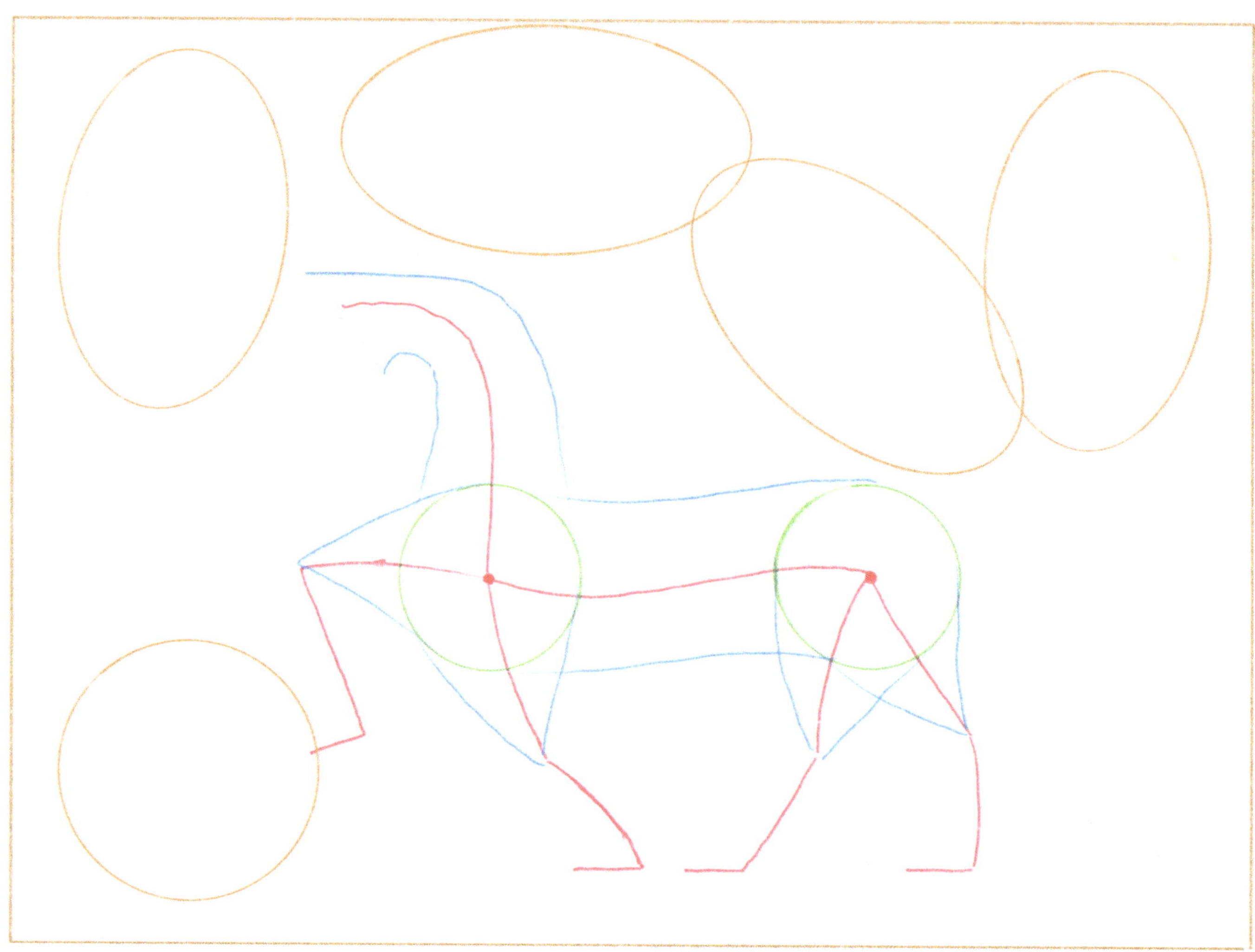

Compositional Areas of Interest

Now that the centrepiece of the composition is in place go on to sketch the placement of surrounding elements.

Ensure that there is room for all the ornamental motifs added to the ribbons of the knotwork pattern later. Take note of the empty spaces between the animal's outline and the bounding box of the canvas. Consider what motifs you want to incorporate and where.

Roughly mark the areas where you want to place the clusters of foliage, palmettes and other ornamental motifs.

In this example, the beast will have a large headpiece shooting off from the top of its head, and its tail will sway forward over its back and fan out in a palmette. A vine will grow from its base at the bottom left corner, encircling the beast and unfurling in foliage in the top corners.

These essential elements need to be considered and made space for

upfront. Other elements like offshoots and leaves can be added later to fill smaller empty spots wherever necessary.

You might not already know by now where your secondary ribbons will go. Don't worry; mark areas of interest where potential ornaments could go for now. Revise this step when you've laid out your secondary ribbons, and edit your marked areas to fit the composition.

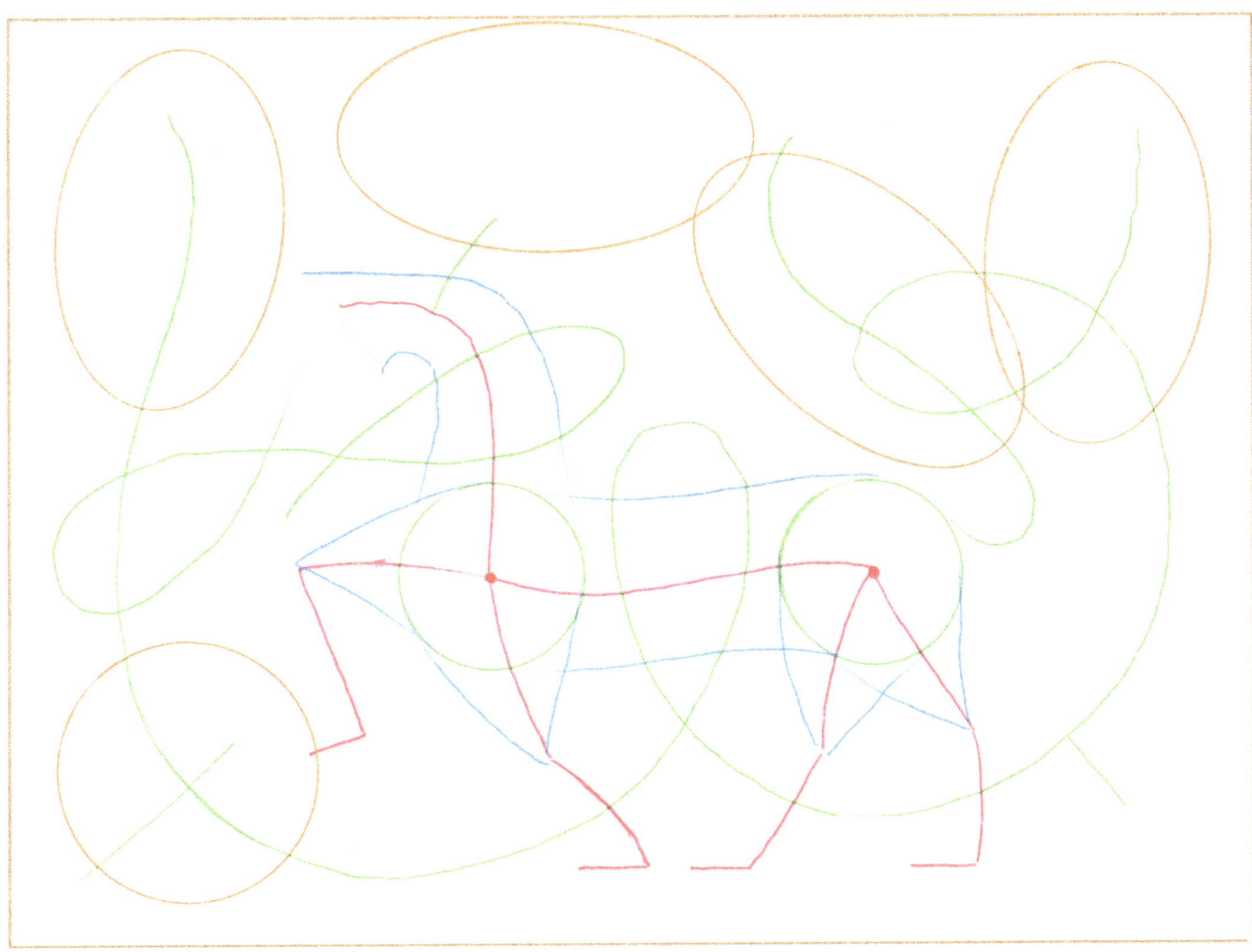

Vine and Serpent:
Ribbon Flow

The secondary ribbons are composed of the beast's tail and the stem of its headpiece, a large vine, and a lesser serpent.

The crest piece will have several tertiary ribbon offshoots from its base, so it's only marked here by a short line from the top of the beast's head.

The tail immediately makes a U-turn and sways into an S-curve going forward above the animal's back.

The vine curls around most of the remaining empty canvas area in curly loops wrapping around the beast's stomach while also interlacing with the legs of the animal.

The serpent ribbon is composing a figure-eight curling around the neck of the beast and the upright stem of the vine.

Try out a couple of different constellations and combinations of secondary ribbons before you settle on a solution. You probably won't get them right in the first go. Play around and experiment with the flow and placements of the ribbons.

Remember that secondary ribbons flow in curly-loop patterns or figure-eights, and to keep it simple with many shorter ribbons rather than a few long ribbons.

Arranging the Tertiary Ribbons

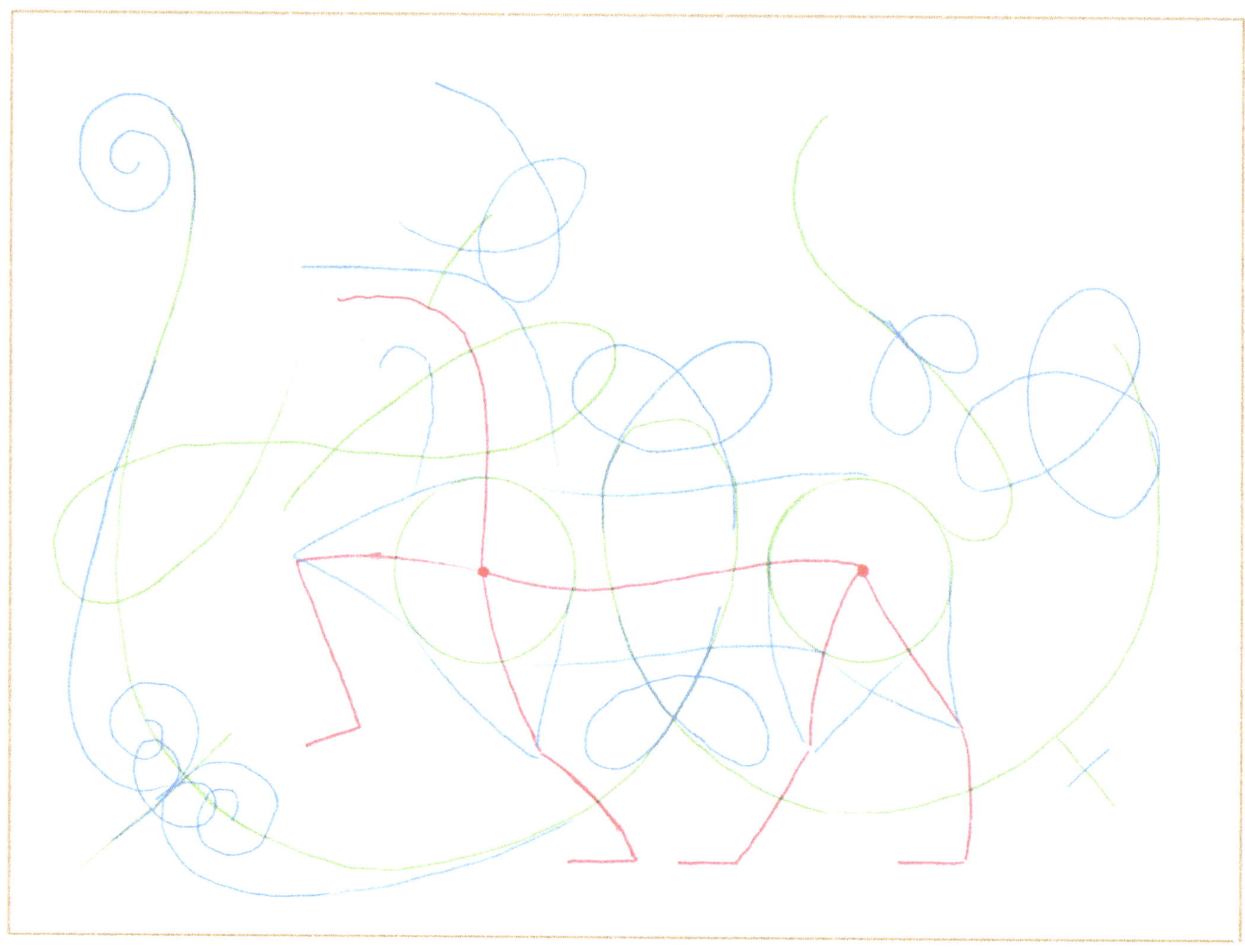

Offshoots: Knots and spirals

Building on the structure of the secondary ribbons, it's time to add tertiary ribbons in the shape of knots and spirals to create mechanisms for offshoots throughout your design.

Add pretzel knots, triquetras, fleur-de-lis, union knots and spirals at select strategic places depending on the mechanism necessary to convey your intentions. Spin them around and try out different options to see what fits best.

In this example, a pretzel knot composes the base of the beast's crest, and a union knot ties together and conveys the tail's palmette of fanning tendrils.

The vine's base comprises two inverse spirals held together by a union knot, with each coil sprouting a stem.

The vertical stem terminates in an additional spiral in the top left corner.

The horisontal stem wraps around the beast in a curly loop. Adding a pretzel knot at the top of the loop and one at

the intersection of the ribbon creates a double pretzel knot motif with the beast's body as the midline running through the double knot.

A fleur-de-lis motif shooting off the branch in the bottom right corner mirrors the union knot at the vine's base to the left.

Finally, the stem terminates in a triquetra knot, entangling the beast's tail in one of its loops.

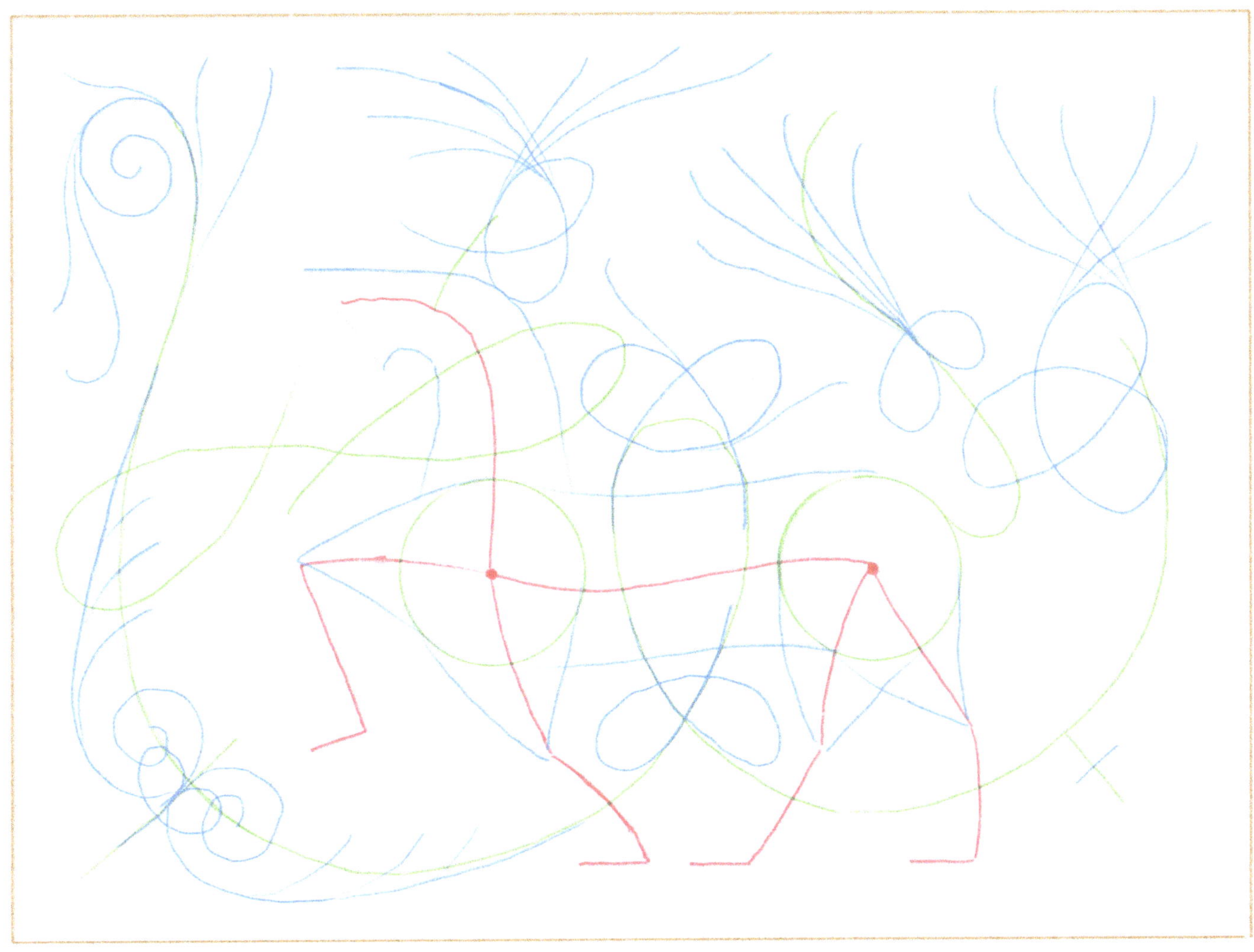

Tendrils: Ribbon Leaves and Terminals

Now that the knots and spirals are in place, you want to get a sense of how the offshoots they produce will fill out the background between the primary and secondary ribbons.

Sketch in the strands of the ribbon terminals for the offshoots, fans and feathers, and the shapes of lobes and leaves.

The crest's pretzel knot sprouts numerous bifurcations, most of them either forward- or backward-facing. The tendrils of the tail fan out on both sides of a centre union knot lobe.

Feathering occurs along the stem on each side of the vine's base. Tendrils unfurl centrifugally from the spiral in the top left corner. The double pretzel knot sprouts a leaf here and there, filling the empty spaces. And finally, the top loop of the vine's triquetra knot grows a tuft of braided tendrils.

These additions to the composition may influence the ribbon flow. Some areas might be much denser than others. Even out the distribution of the tendrils by adjusting the design elements accordingly, either by thinning out the number of tendrils or shifting the position of specific components.

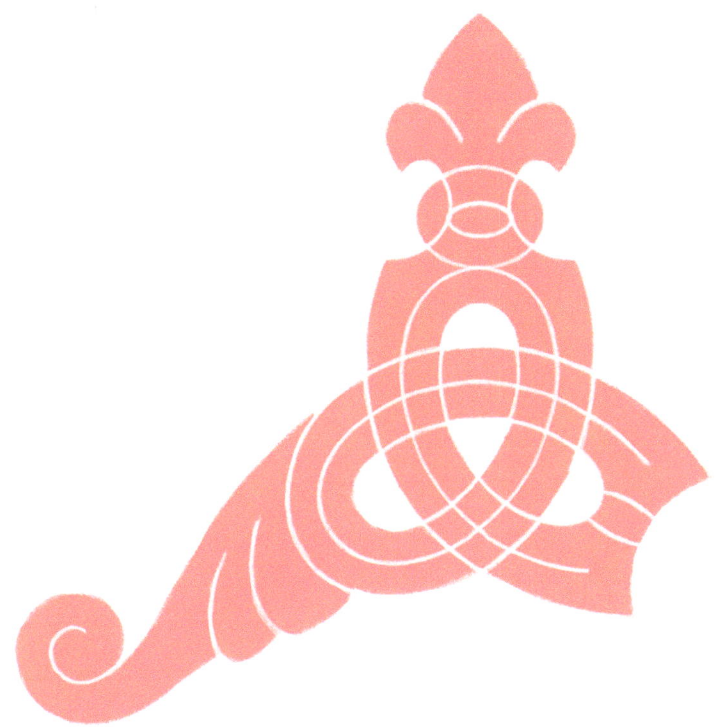

Modelling and Sculpting the Design

This phase will sculpt the shapes and details of the design so that any issues have been ironed out before rendering your design.

On top of the foundational structure of the ribbon flow, you'll flesh out the width of the ribbons to begin giving shape to the composition. You'll add more definition by sculpting the ornamental motifs, focusing on their silhouettes to balance shapes and white space. Lastly, you'll draw the contours of all the ribbons, tendrils and leaves to articulate the details of the design.

Adding Ribbon Widths

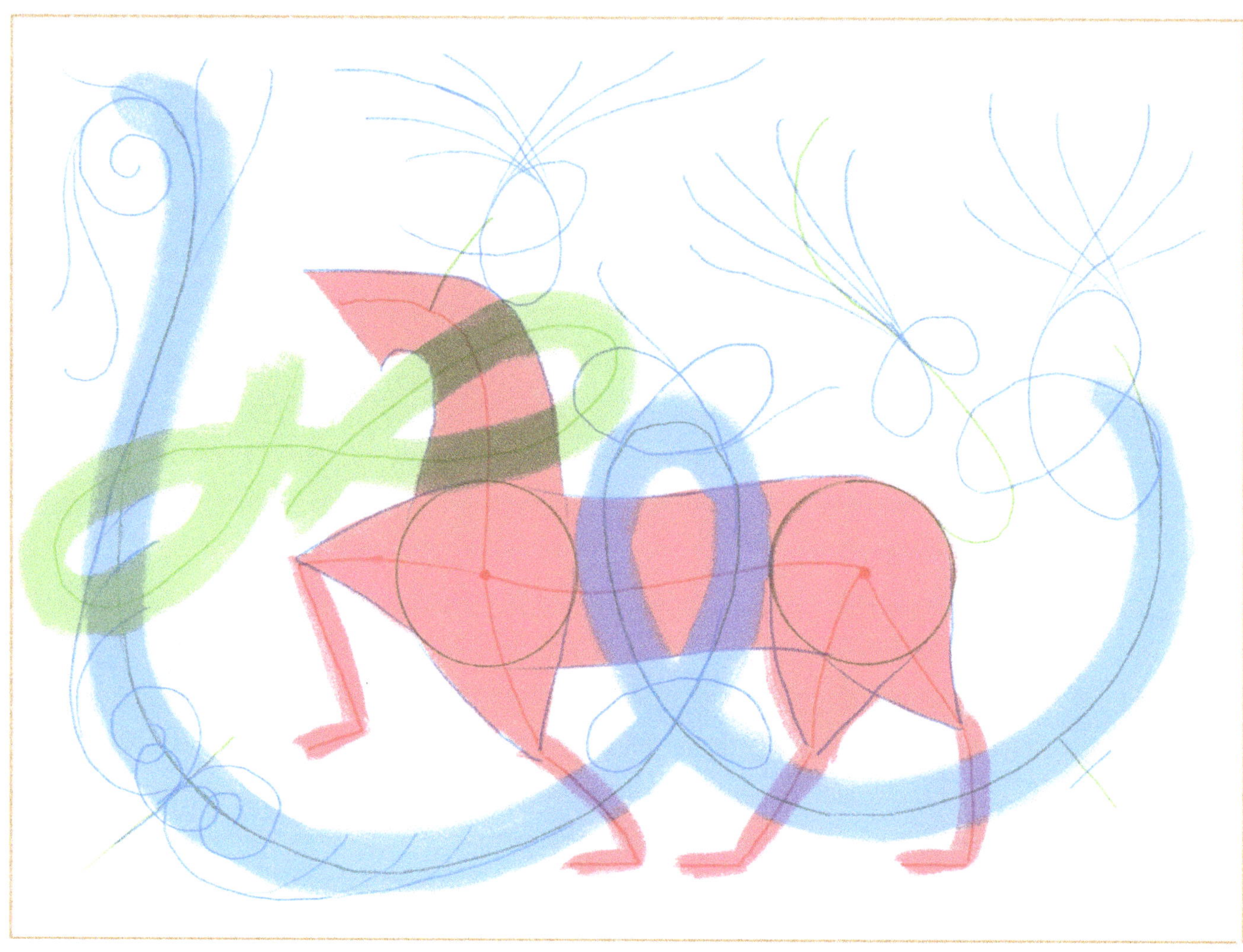

Primary Ribbon Widths

Roughly fill in the beast's body and legs, that you outlined earlier.

The thighs taper from the outline of the hip spiral's circumference into the knees, where it bends and continues in an even ribbon width, similar to the tertiary ribbons, towards the ankles. Fill in the rough shape of the feet too.

Don't be afraid to readjust the stance or reconfigure limbs to better fit in with the interlacing ribbons of the surrounding vine and serpent.

Secondary Ribbon Widths

Add width to the secondary ribbons by filling in the ribbon with colour. This applies to the stem of the vine and the serpent's body.

You want to keep the ribbon width even throughout, with only a few exceptions, for example, at the broader spiral base of the vine, from where it tapers into the general ribbon width.

Make sure there is enough space between ribbons, especially in places of tight interlace. You want to weave the ribbons somewhat snugly while keeping the uniform ribbon widths without squeezing any of the interlacing strands.

Keep the ribbons flowing smoothly in even curves. You probably have to adjust the ribbon flow here and there to make up for the added width.

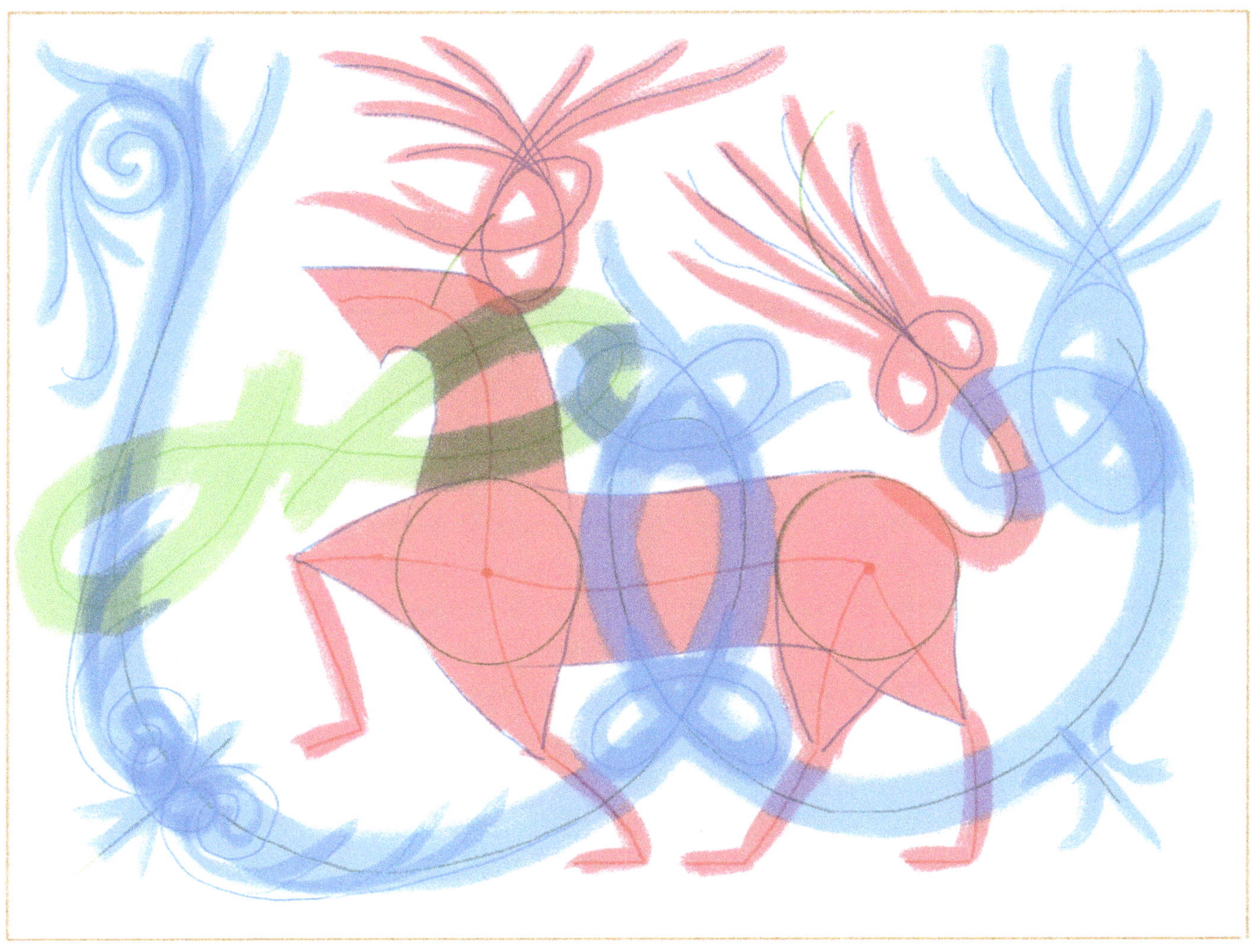

Tertiary Ribbon Widths

Go on to add in the widths of tertiary ribbons used for the knots and spirals and their tendril offshoots.

Areas of focus in this example are the beast's crest and tail and the knots and spirals along the vine's stem.

Keep in mind that the width of the tertiary ribbons is roughly half the size of the secondary ribbons.

Adjustments

Glance across the entire composition and make a note of any possible imbalances.

Make sure that the width of the beast's body compliments the widths of the other ribbons and that the animal's interaction with the surrounding compositional elements feels organic.

All the ribbons, loops and knots of the composition should feel like they are evenly distributed across the surface, and there should be enough space between the strands in the knots and loops of interlacing ribbons.

You might also find that you need to shift the beast slightly to one side, tilt the vines a bit to balance the composition, scale some of the bigger knots and ribbons down or up in size or move them a bit to make more space for the tendril terminals.

Now's your last chance to make adjustments to the overall composition before we move into focusing on shaping the details.

Sculpting the Ornamental Motifs

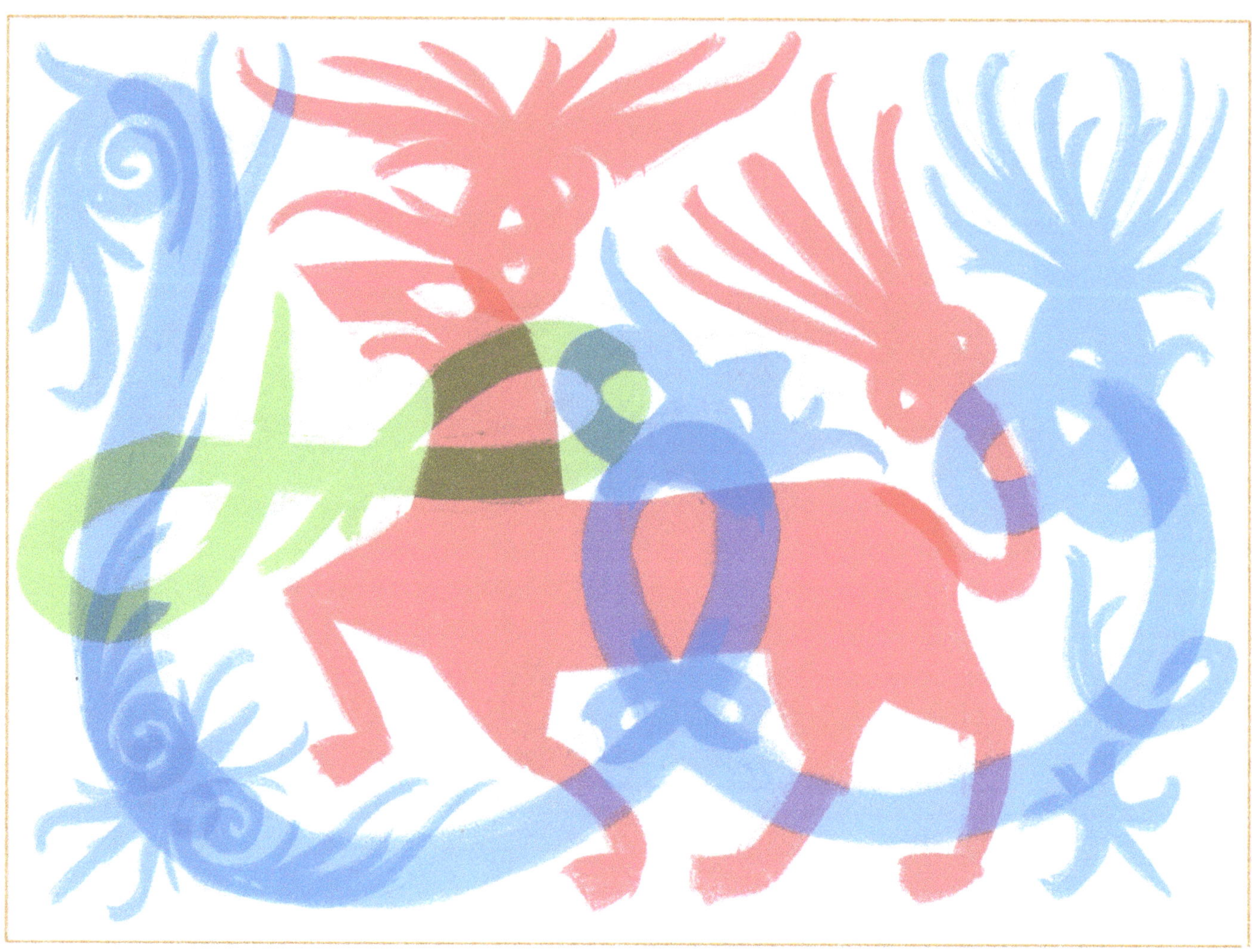

Rough Shapes

Now that you have a good sense of the ribbon flow throughout the composition, we'll shift the focus to shaping a harmonious silhouette for each of the compound elements like the beast's crest and the other individual knotwork pieces and the more figurative elements like animal heads.

At this stage, you want to be aware of each of the tendril terminals and roughly where they go without locking them in completely. Ensure acanthus leaves and tendrils flow in even S-curves across the board. Keep a light hand, and don't be afraid to experiment, edit and change things around as you go to make the design feel more organic.

Shape the beast's head silhouette by carving out the eye and the mouth. Shape up the legs and feet too. Reshape and adjust the overall silhouette of the crest- and tailpieces and define structural elements like the centre lobe and the width of feathering ribbons.

Work your way along the vine's stem, adding the fleur-de-lis's shape in the bottom right corner. Create a balanced silhouette for the base and sketch in the spirals, the feathering along the stems, and the union knot with its protruding leaves. Go to the terminal at the top and sketch the spiral there. Roughly sculpt the shape of the loops in the double knot, adding the dents in the loops. Shape the leaves of the braided tuft on the triquetra. Add in offshoots along the stem.

Reshape the serpent and fill in the silhouette of its pointy head and tail.

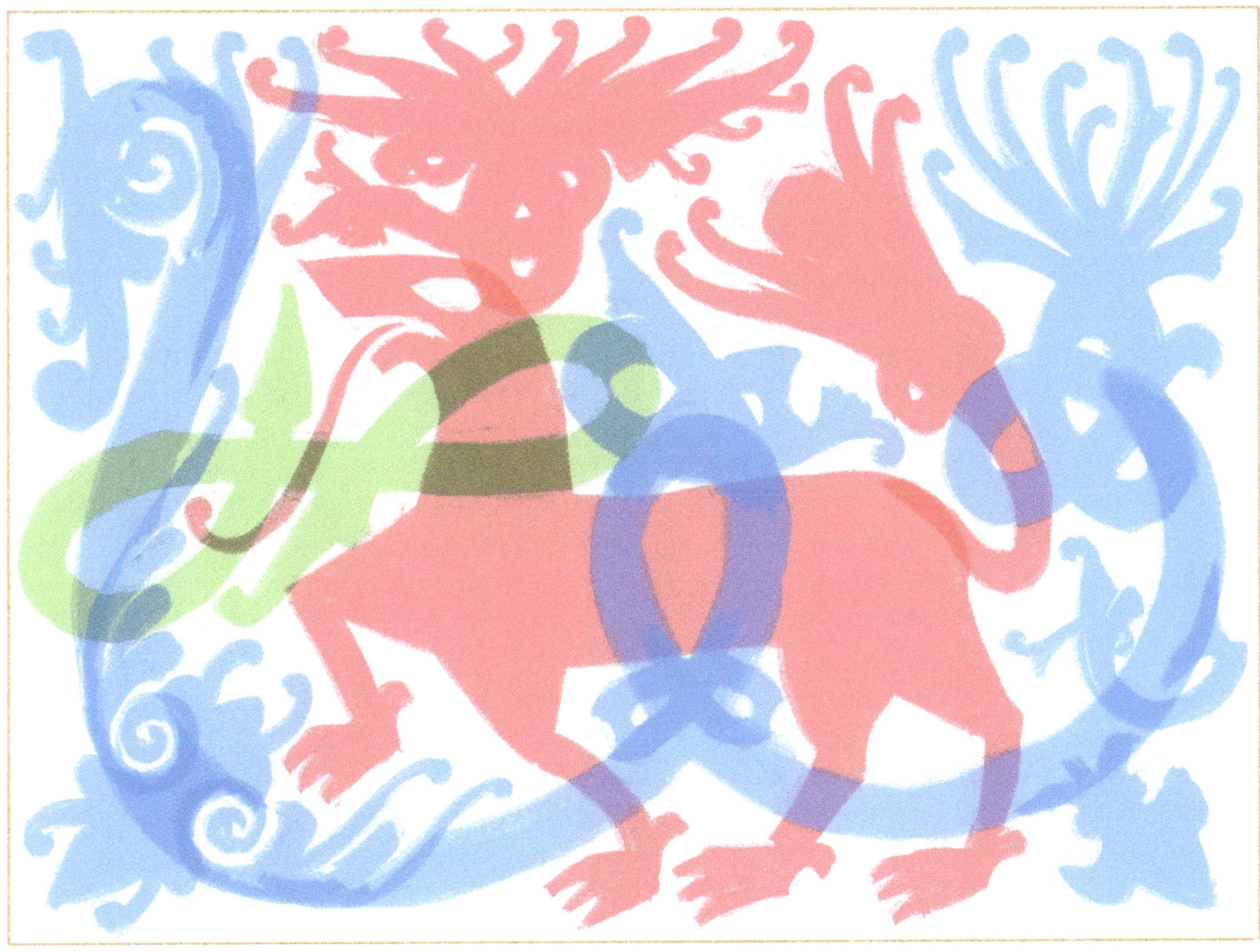

Even Out the Kinks

It's time to go through each ornamental motif and shape them more accurately. Add all the minor details and flourishes like ball terminals and side lobes to the acanthus leaves and carve out indents to selected loops.

Keep an eye on the proportions of repeating elements. The size of leaves and tendril terminals should stay relatively uniform and stick to roughly one or two sizes throughout the design to make it look cohesive and feel deliberate.

Work on the silhouette of the shapes of knots, ribbons and leaves to create exciting and complementary elements playing well together in the composition. Make sure there's an even balance between the ornamental motifs and the empty background areas.

Begin with the beast. Add terminal balls to the crest's and tail's leaf terminals and articulate the feathering. Add the claws and spurs to the feet. Add an S-curved tongue rolling out the beast's mouth. Articulate all the leaves and lobes around the base of the vine

and the feathering along each of the stems. Add ball terminals and lobes to the leaves and tendrils of the vertical stem's spiral. Shape the leaves of the double knot wrapping around the beast. Articulate the silhouette of the fleur-de-lis in the bottom left corner with its side and centre lobes and the ring around their stems. Shape the loop and acanthus leaves of the offshoot and add the dent in the loop where it's connected to the stem. Add terminal balls to the braided tuft's tendril leaves on top of the triquetra. Shape the silhouette of the serpent's head and tail.

Carving out the Contours

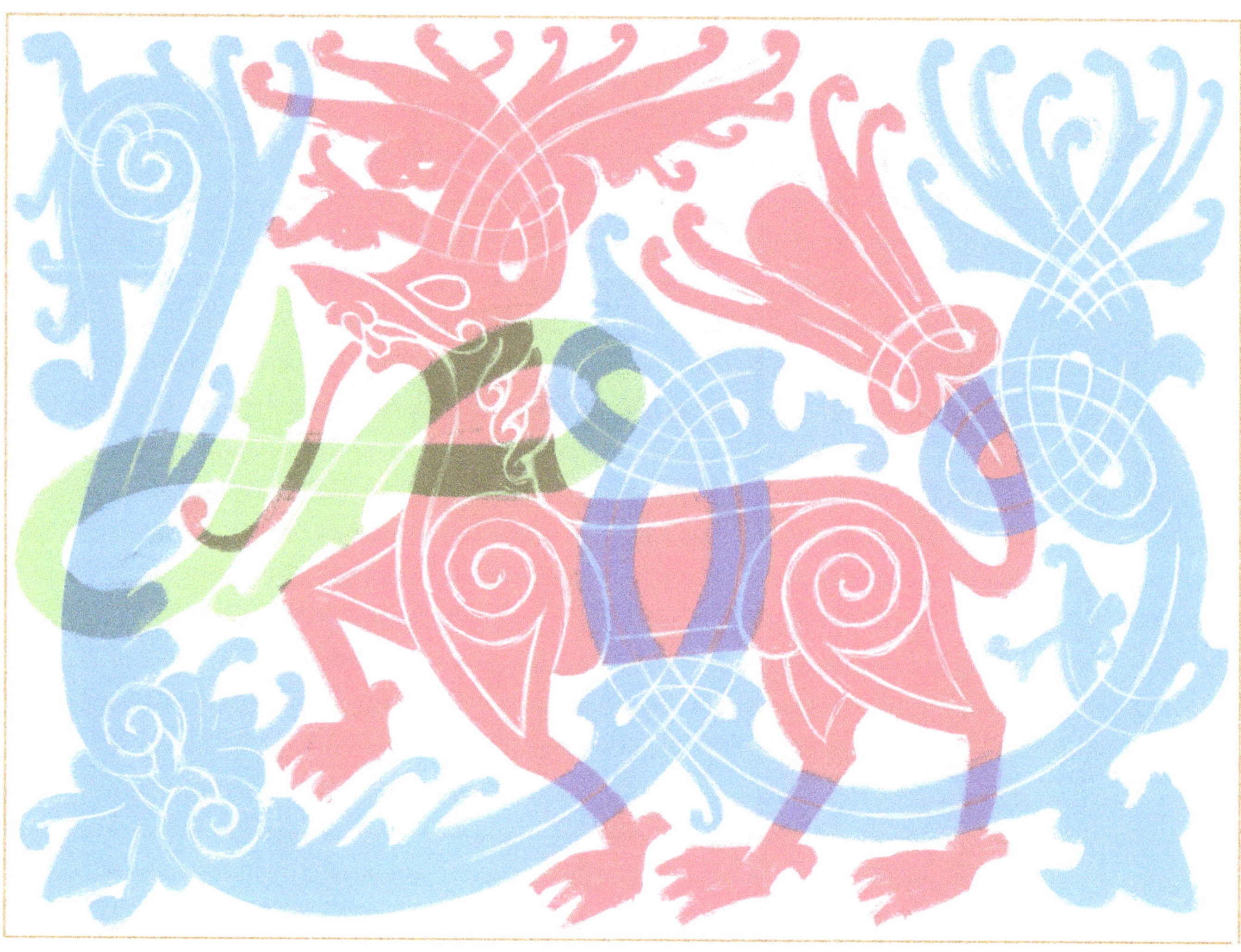

Inner Contour Lines

Sketch in the linework of the inner ribbon contours of the silhouettes.

Make sure every ribbon of every interlacing knot and loop flows meticulously in and out of each other. Adjust the flow and width of ribbons wherever needed.

It's crucial to lock down the inner workings of the ribbons first, as their dimensions are the foundation of all the other tendril offshoots in the design building upon them.

Draw in the beast's inner outlines; the coiling spiral hips, hip lobes and the triangular contour of the thighs. Fill in the beast's facial features; the lip lappet, teeth and inner almond-shaped eye. Go on to trace the inner outline of the ribbons of the various loops and knots throughout the design. Begin with the pretzel knot of the beast's crest and the union knot of its tail. Finish the inner outlines of the beast by adding in the acanthus leaf-shaped hair locks of the mane.

Go through the knots, loops and spirals of the vine. Trace in the midline dividing the double-stranded stem. Follow it through in the pretzel knots tied around the beast's body and the triquetra knot at the end with its braided tendrils on top. Draw in the lines of the spiral base and the spiral terminal and its curling tendril leaves, loops and offshoots.

Lastly, mark the outline of the serpent's body where it overlaps itself.

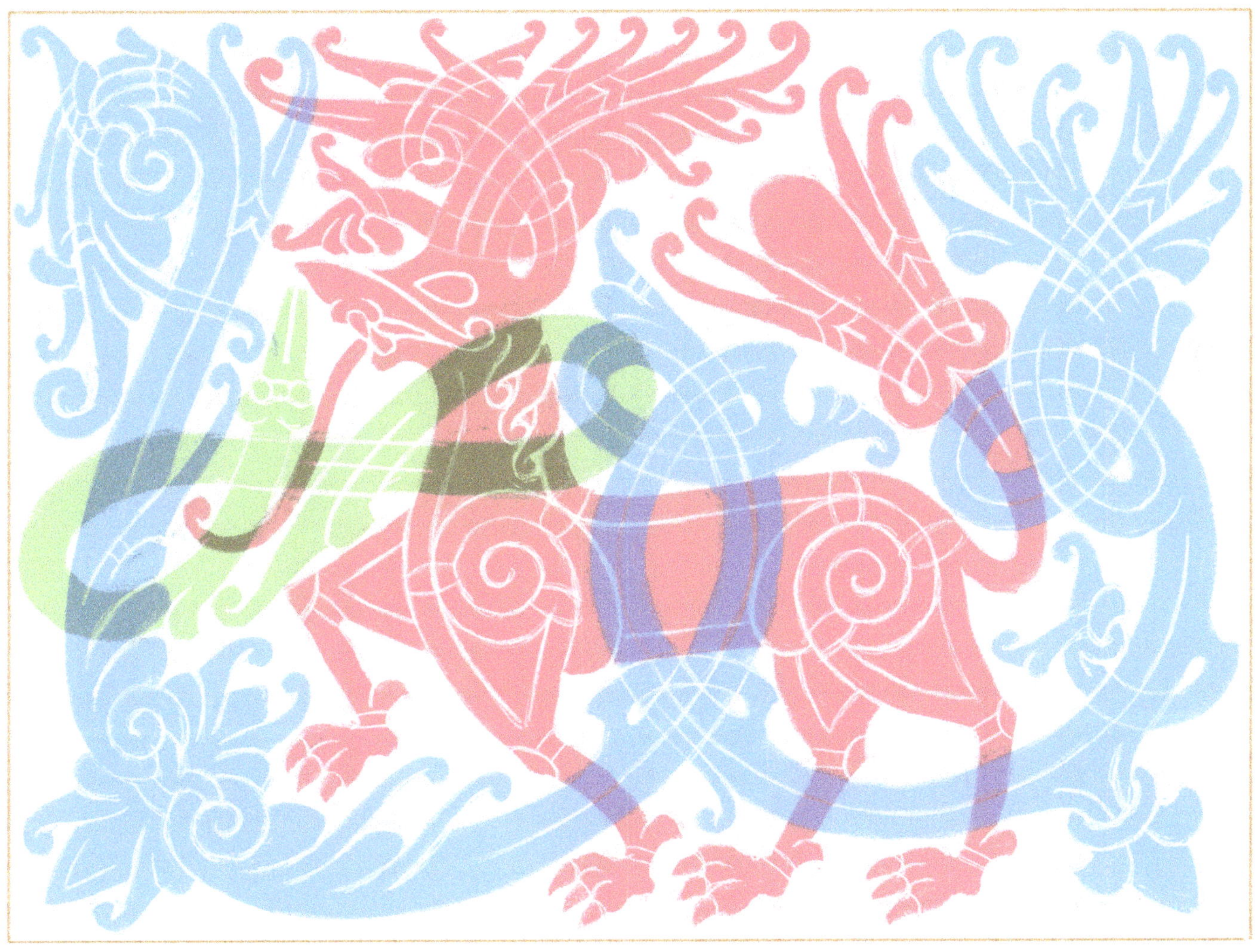

Outer Contour Lines

Now that the inner contours of the ribbons of knots, spirals and animal body parts are articulated, you can draw the outlines of the outer, more free-flowing elements like the tendril terminals, fleur-de-lis motifs, and palmettes as well as add in overlaying details like ribbon snippets.

Build on the inner structure of the ornamental motifs you articulated in the previous step and add the details on top of these. In this round, you can add many small flourishes and details

to personalise your design. Some elements might not have turned out as you expected them to. Don't be afraid still to try out alternative design solutions for knots and motifs. Add an extra leaf or a ribbon snippet here and there as you please. Change things around until they fit well together.

Draw in the details of the beast's headpiece and tail, and add in the ribbon snippets of the spiral hips and the details of the knee joints and feet.

Work your way through the vine, articulating each leaf and lobe of the

base with its union knot and fleur-de-lis motifs. Go on to shape each leaf and tendril, curling around the terminal spiral in the top left corner. Some leaves and tendrils might loop around each other or interlace with the stem and other surrounding tendrils. Carve out each of the tendril-terminal leaves in the braided top of the triquetra knot at the other end of the vine and every loop, offshoot, and lobe in between the two ends.

Fill in the details of the serpent's head and tail.

The Finishing Touches

All the groundwork is now done, and you've figured out all the ins and outs of the design, so now you're ready to sand off the kinks and give it a nice coat of paint and polish.

First, you'll do the finishing touches by defining how the ribbons weave in and out of each other by erasing the hidden outlines to make a nice and clean reference for inking. Then you'll add in possible last details and edits. You'll render the design by inking in the contouring linework and colour in the foreground and background to make the figures stand out.

Weaving the Ribbons

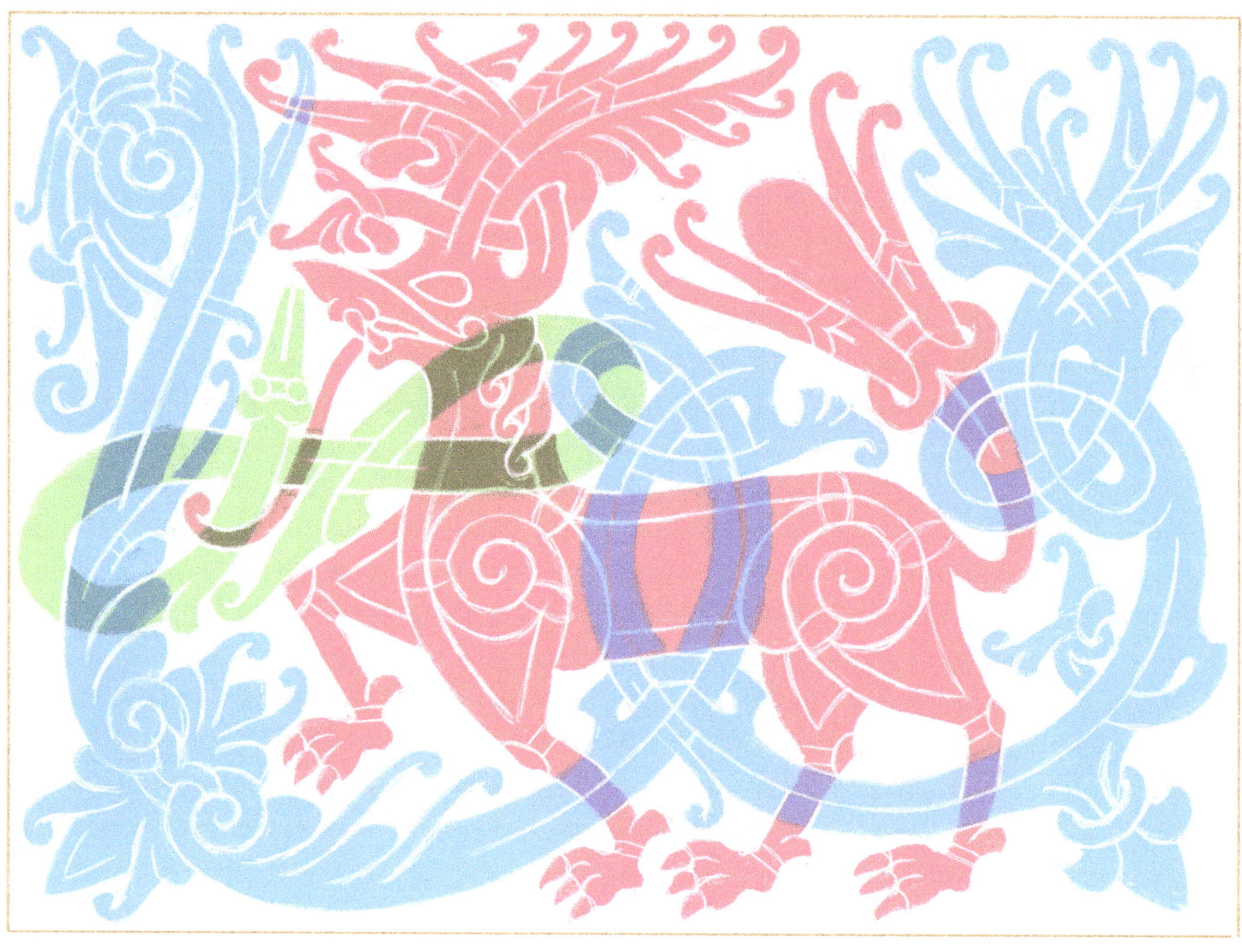

Weaving

Now that you have everything sketched out and shaped up nicely, the only thing you need to do before inking and colouring is to define the weave of the interlacing ribbons.

Select an intersection where you already know which ribbon goes on top of the other and start from there.

You might, for example, want the top of the neck of the beast to be on top of the serpent's tail to make space for the head to stand out a little better.

Work your way from your chosen intersection, erase all the lines of hidden ribbons, and draw in the outlines of overlapping strands.

Ensure the ribbons keep alternating between going under and over intersecting ribbons and strands.

Usually, it will all magically add up. But occasionally, it just doesn't. You might have an offshoot somewhere, adding an uneven number of tendrils to the weave, which throws off the rhythm. That's ok; then you'll adjust the interlacing pattern, probably by adding

an extra offshoot to the mix to even out the number of ribbons. Or, you can just accept that it didn't add up and move on, leaving two occasional strands going over or under in a row.

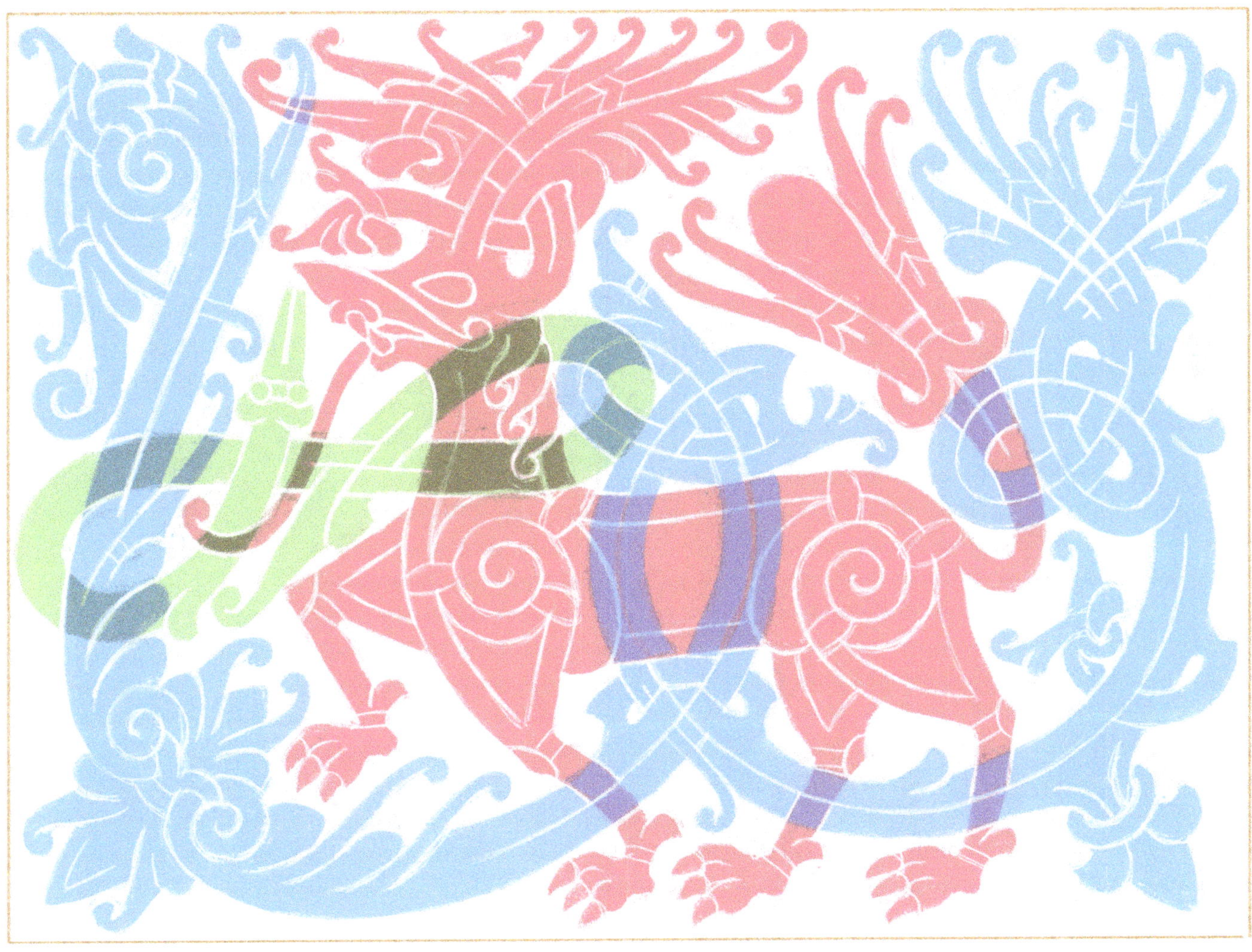

Final Adjustments

That's it. Your design is now fully fledged.

Lean back and let your eye wander over the composition. Is something sticking out? Now's your last chance to add a lobe to fill an empty spot, rearrange a few tendrils or even out the proportions of specific details.

In this example, I shortened a tendril leaf in the vertical stem's spiral terminal, added a lobe to the triquetra knot, elongated a tendril in the crest's feathered leaf and readjusted the serpent's left loop and surrounding tendrils.

Inking and Colouring

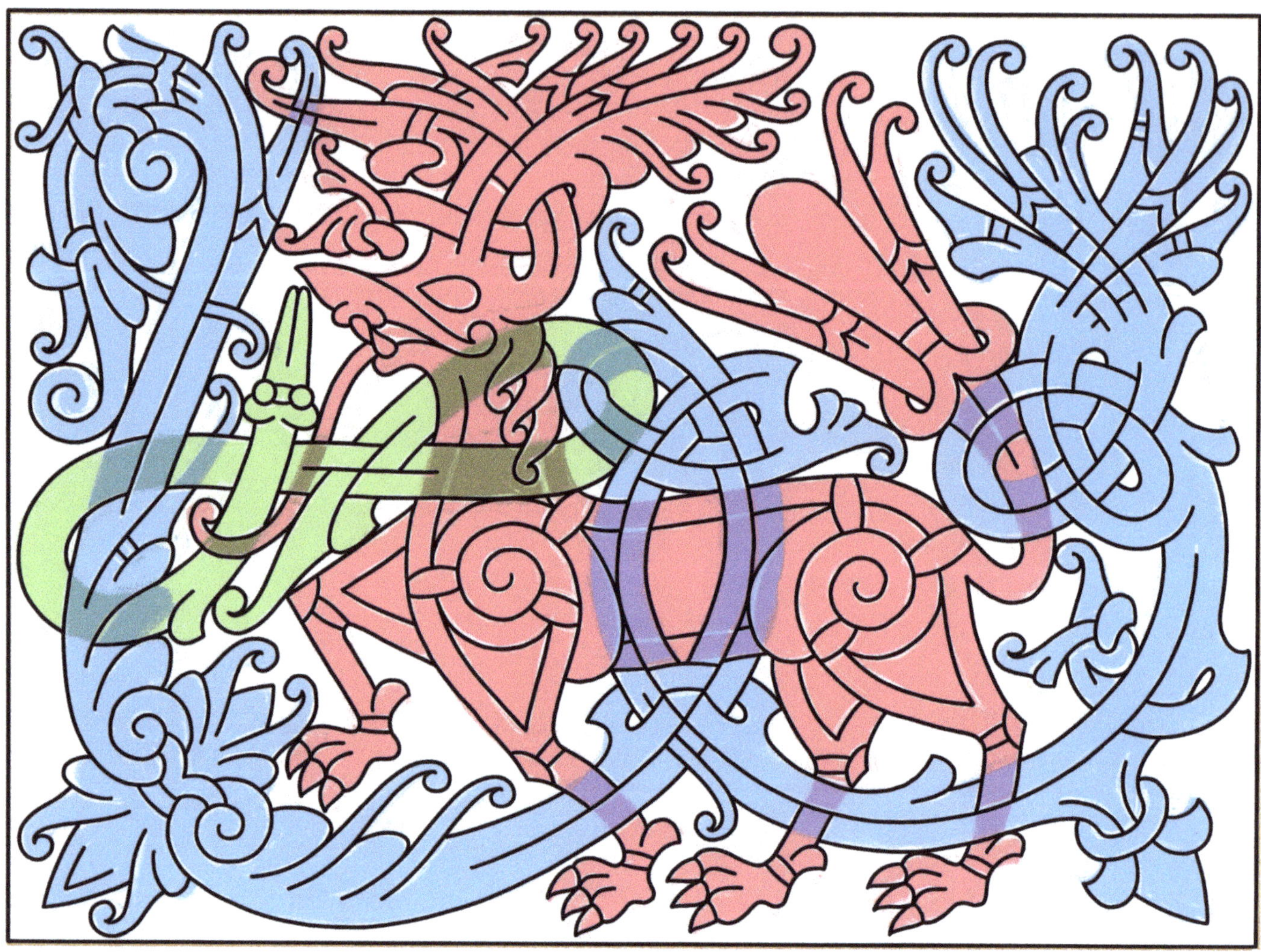

Inking

Now that the design is fully sculpted, it's time to ink the outlines and add colour to the figures and background.

Trace the outline of the ribbons and shapes with a mono-width brush or vectorise the design by penning in the lines in your design app of choice.

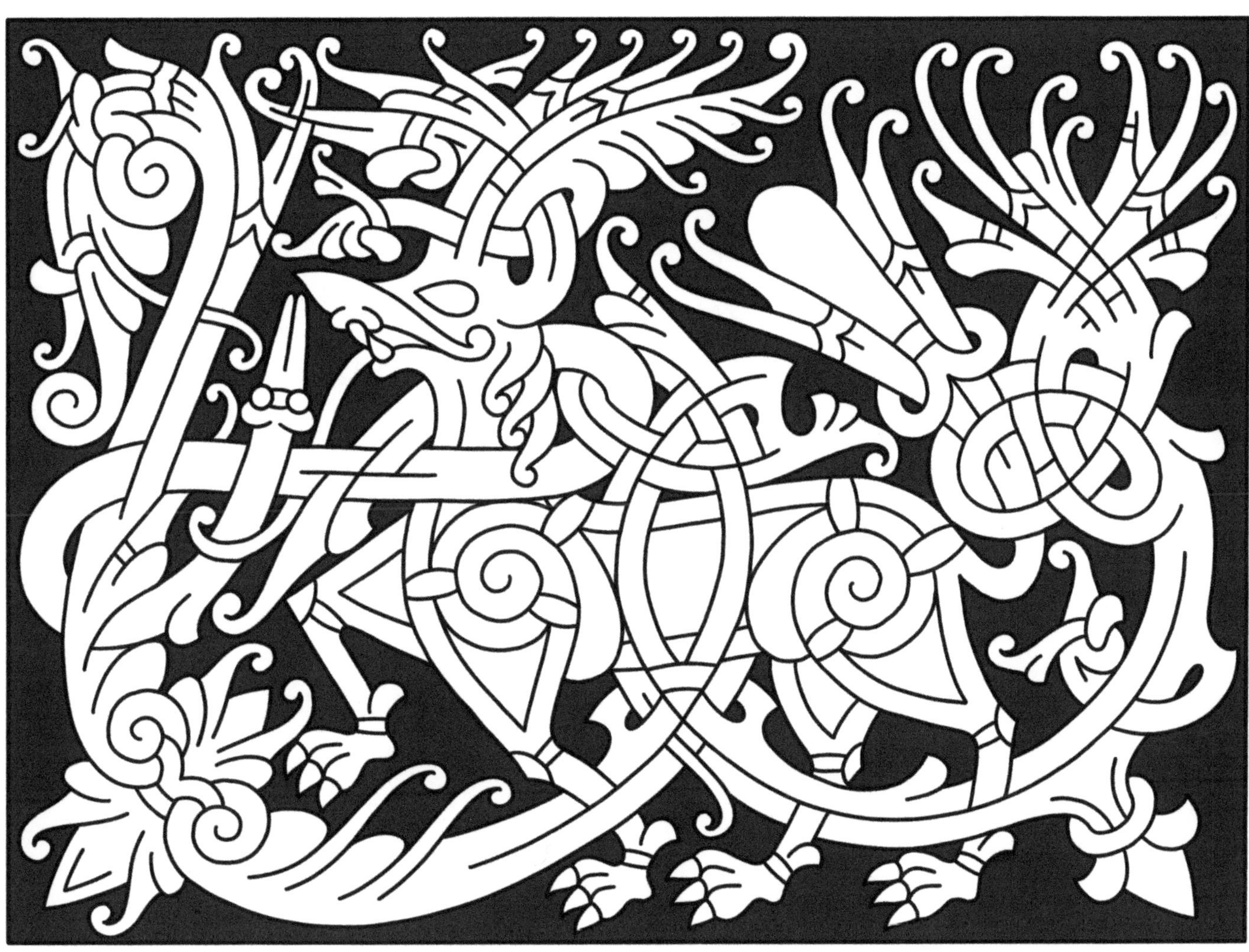

Colouring

In this example, I've done a simple colouring job and painted the background dark grey and coloured the beast, vine and serpent in the same light grey.

But you can style it in various other ways if you like to personalise your design and give it a bit more flare.

You can use more vivid colours and add one or more accent colours for specific details.

Maybe even add textures like dots and hashes. See, for example, the St. Paul's stone and photos of the Cammin and Bamberg caskets for inspiration on how it was done historically.

That's it. Well done! Your design is now finished, and I hope you are happy with the result.

Next Steps

Congratulations!

You've created your own Ringerike-style design true to the original principles.

Best of all, you are now well-equipped to take on any other type of design in the same style.

So what's next?

Recreating Your Design

Hopefully, you're proud of your new creation (as you should be!). But maybe you would like to have done a few things differently if you were to do it again.

Well, good news! You are free to recreate your design, and it might actually be a good idea to really get all your new skills and knowledge to stick.

You might want to try out new variations for your design to explore the possibilities of the style within the boundaries of the great beast motif.

Take a Deep-dive into the Reference Material

If you need a break from drawing, try diving into the original historical references instead. Now that you have a deeper understanding of the style, you might see the artworks in a new light and discover interesting details you didn't recognise before. This will hopefully get you inspired and fired up to get back into drawing.

You might be lucky and be located near a museum with a collection on display. Otherwise, don't sweat; many museums have online collections readily available on the web.

Books are, of course, another great resource. Pay your local library or bookshop a visit and get inspired.

Creating a New Design

Are you inspired to explore what else the Ringerike style has to offer?

Ever wanted to create various other motifs in the same style, like dragons, ravens or the world tree? Well, you're ready for the challenge. You now have the skills and know-how required.

All the principles of knotwork, ornamental motifs and compositional structures you've learned through this book are directly applicable to all other motifs in the Ringerike style.

You only need to look at how these standard building blocks are reconfigured to create other motifs and compositions.

Look at the references at the back of this book to see examples of how other designs are constructed by the same principles.

Thank you for spending your time with me. I hope you feel empowered and eager to take on your next design, and I wish you good luck!

Cheers!

Online Collections

Nationalmuseet
National Museum of Denmark
→ samlinger.natmus.dk

Universitetsmuseene
Norway's University Museums
→ unimus.no/portal

Statens Historiska Museer
National Museums of Sweden
→ samlingar.shm.se

The British Museum
→ britishmuseum.org/collection

References

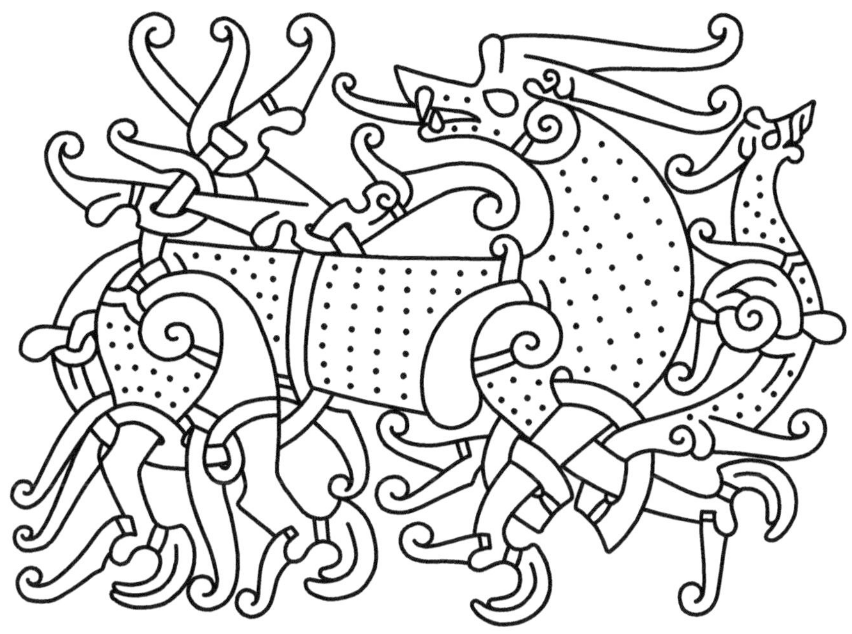

E 2, St Paul's Churchyard, London, England.

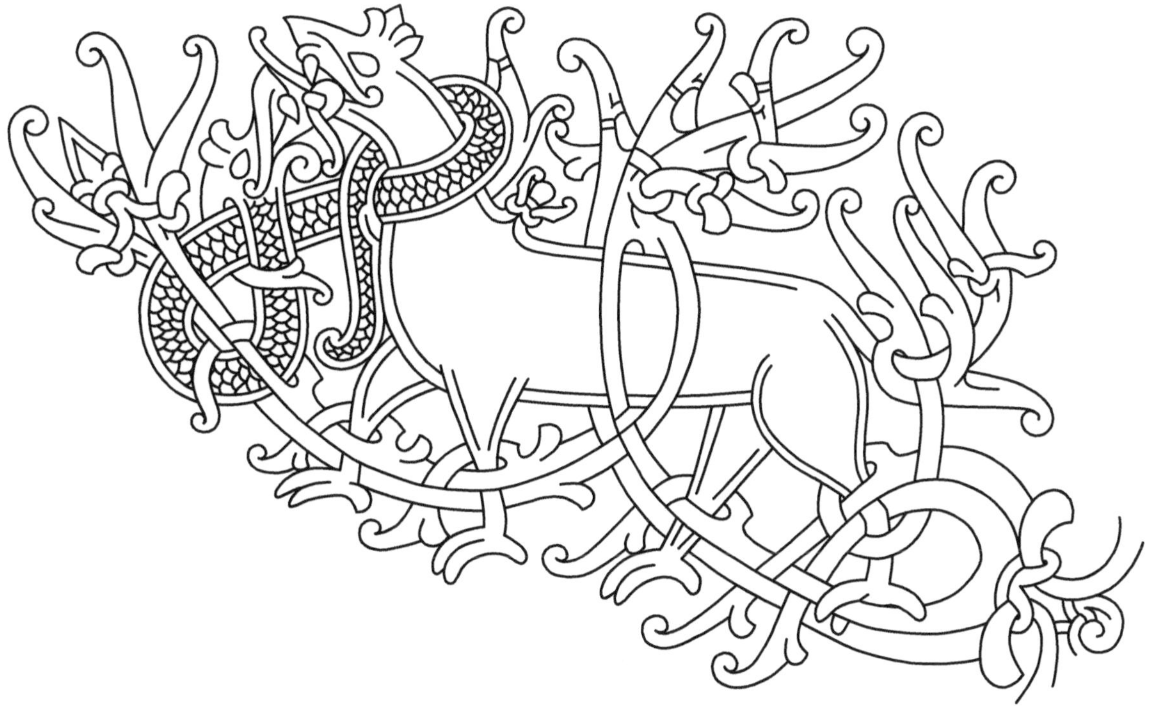

The Källunge weather vane, Sweden.

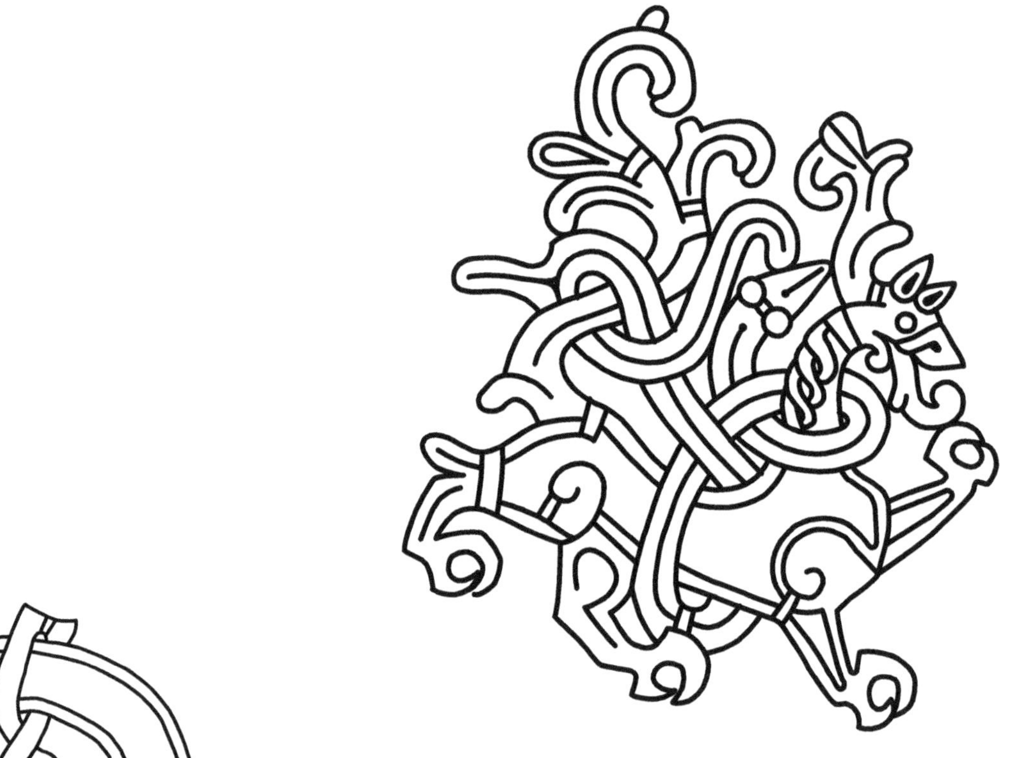

DR 42, The greater Jelling stone, Jelling, Jylland, Denmark.

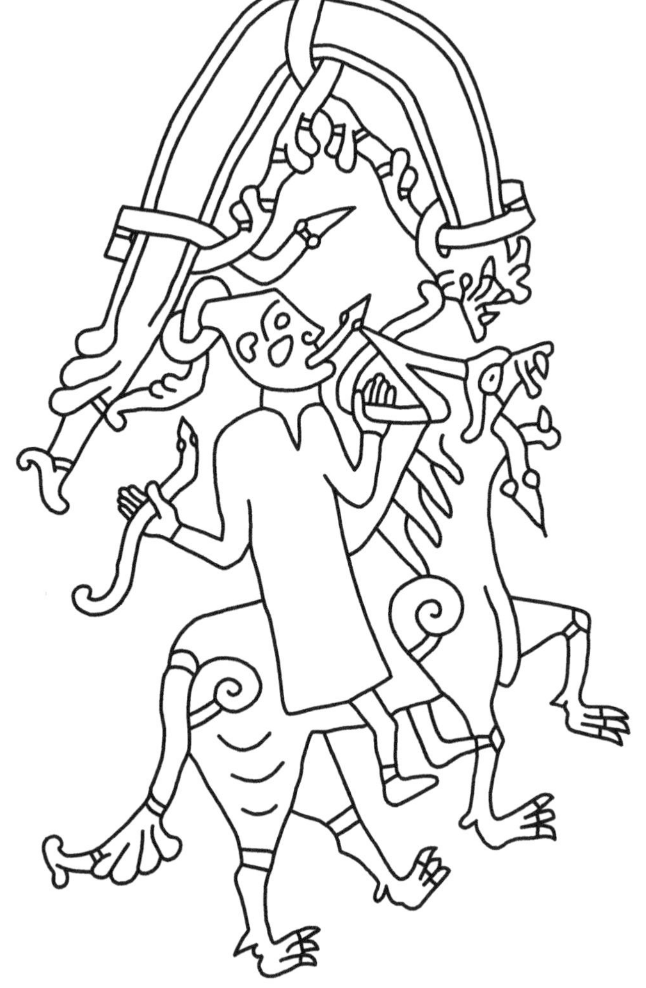

DR 284, Hunnestad, Skåne, Sweden.

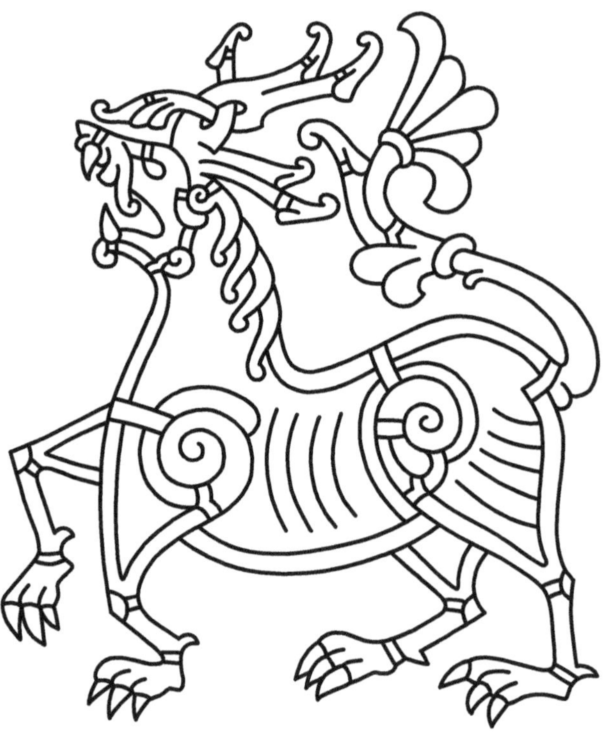

DR 285, Hunnestad, Skåne, Sweden.

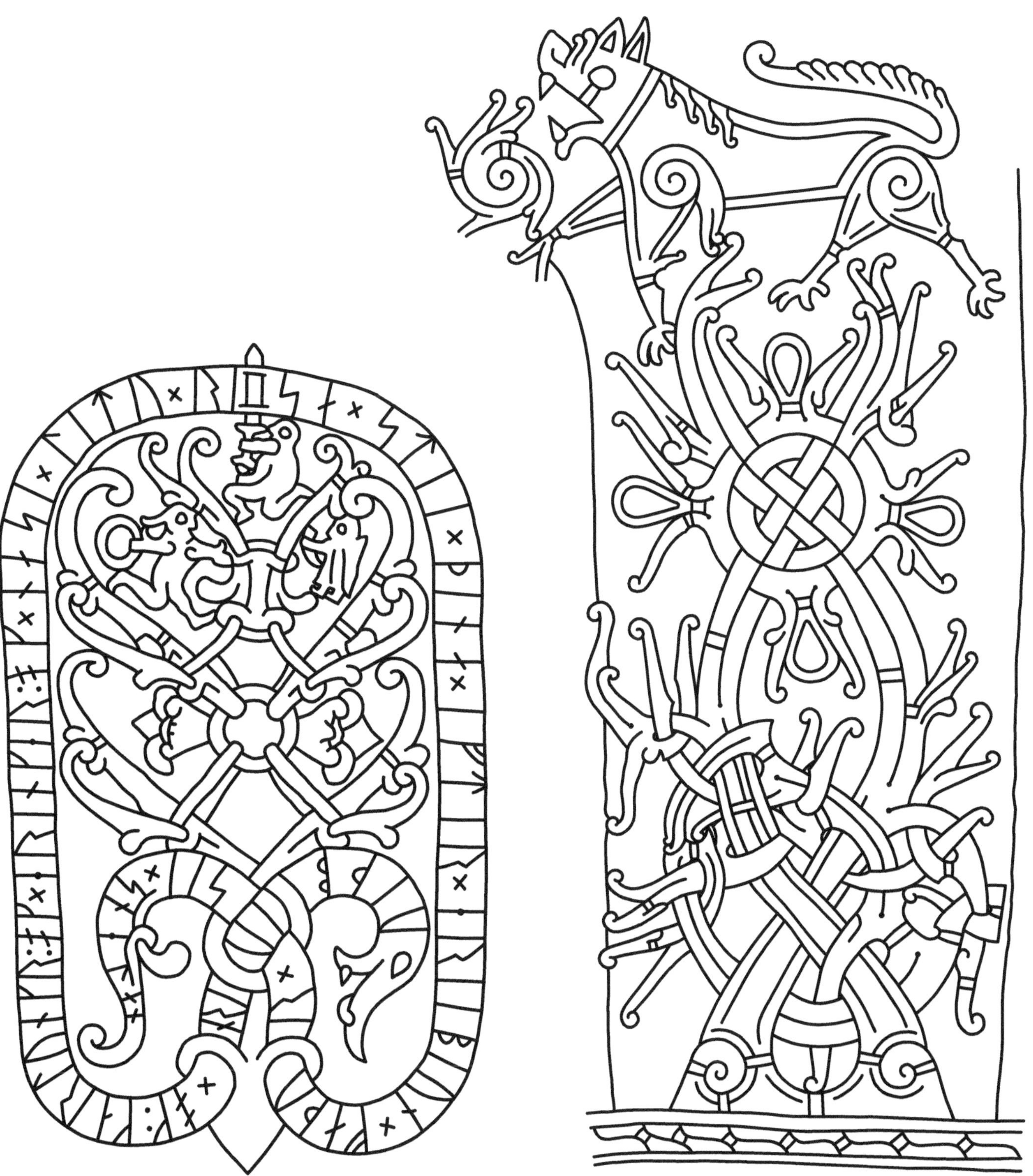

U 1163, Drävle, Uppland, Sweden.

N 61, N 62, Alstad, Oppland, Norway.

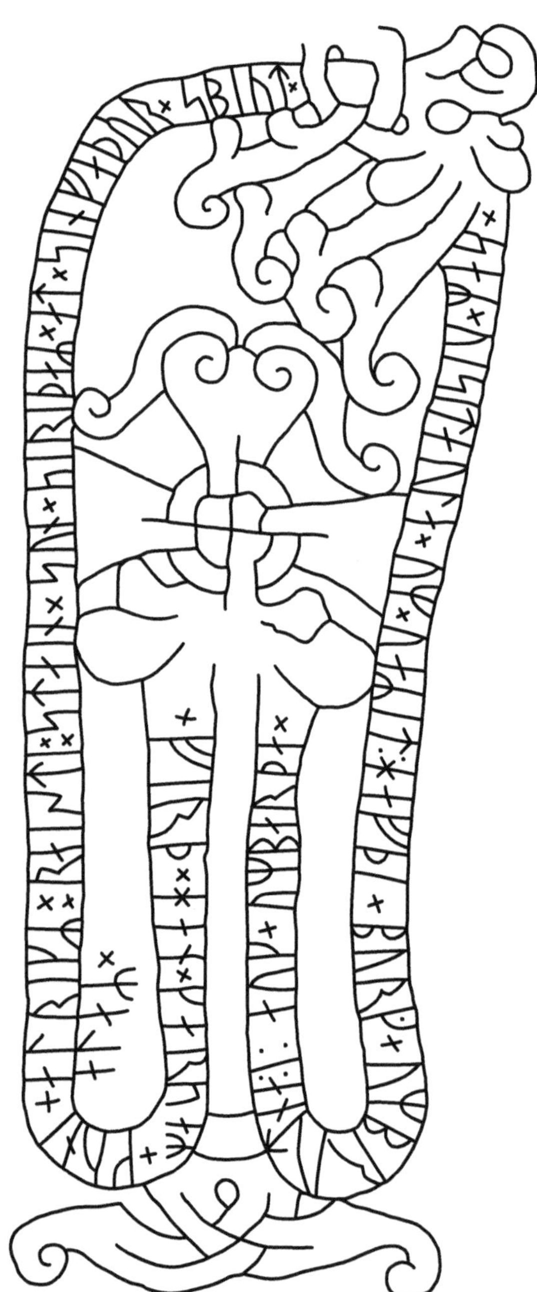

Sö 106, Kungshållet, Södermanland, Sweden.

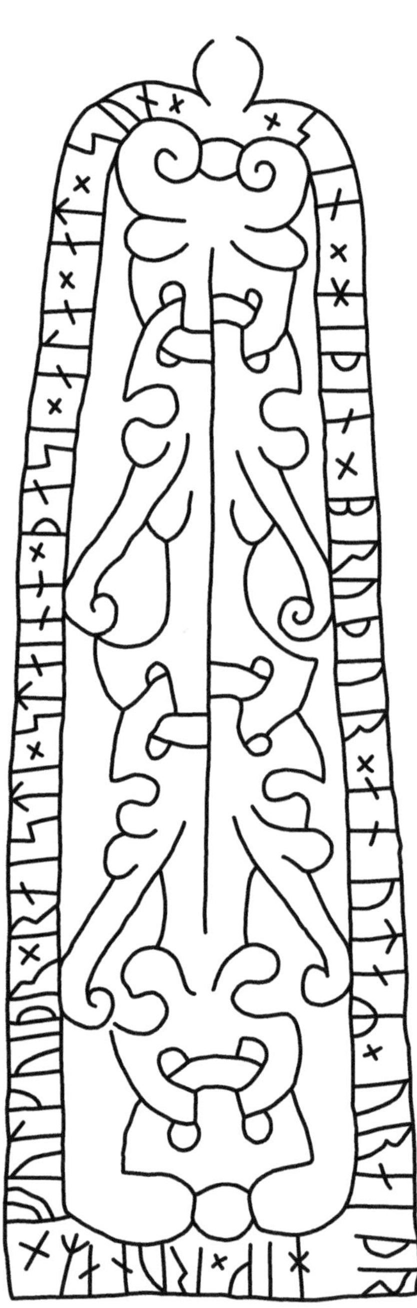

Vs 13, Anundshög, Västmanland, Sweden.

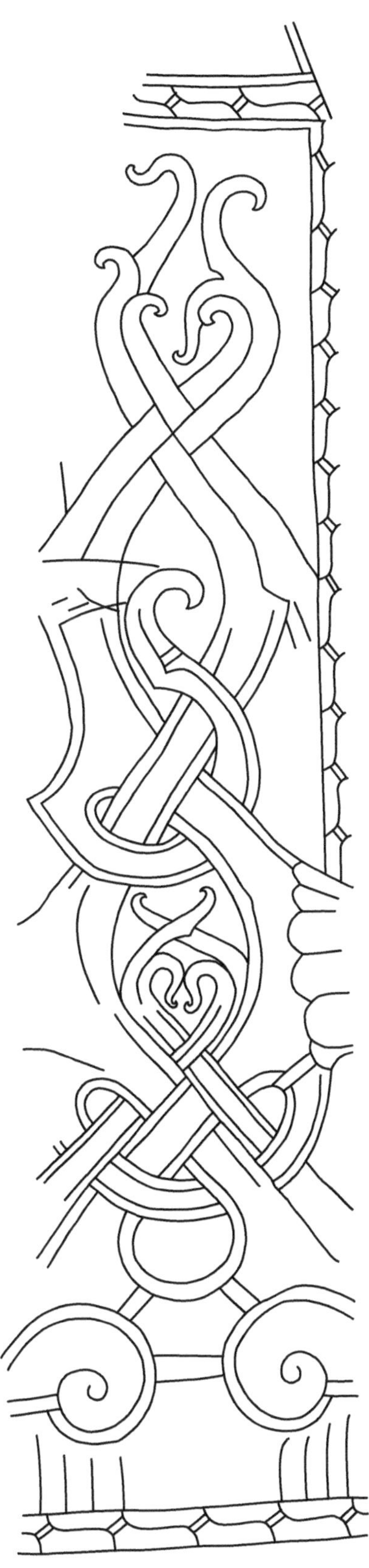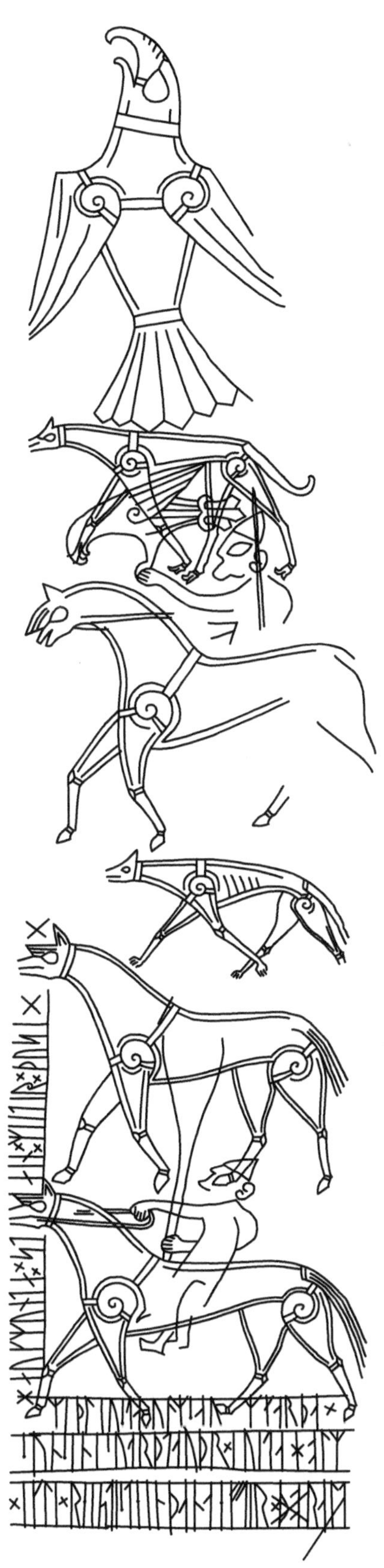

N 84, Vang, Oppland, Norway.

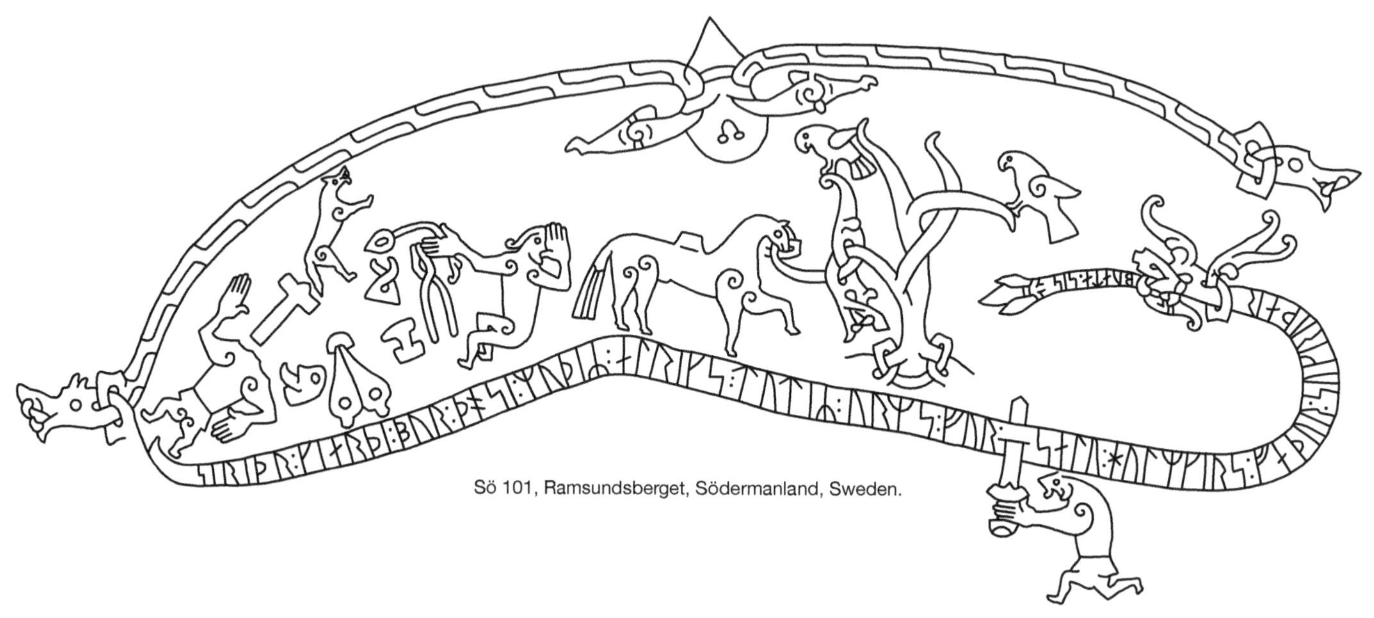

Sö 101, Ramsundsberget, Södermanland, Sweden.

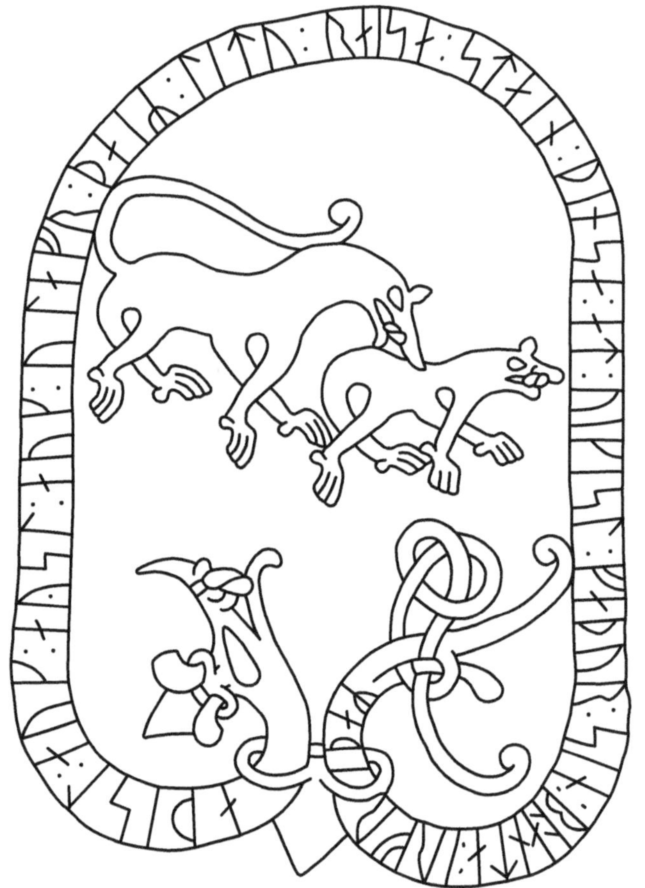
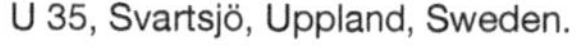

U 35, Svartsjö, Uppland, Sweden.

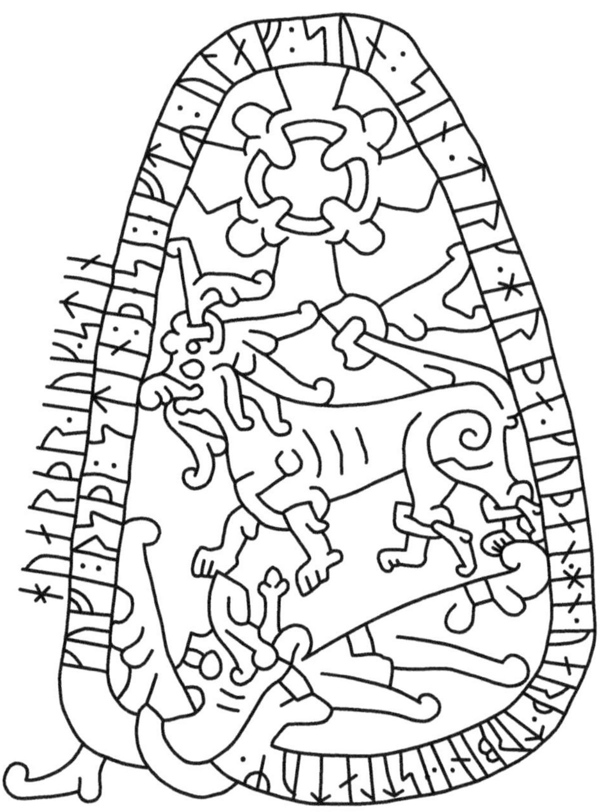

Vg 181, Norra Åsarp, Västergötland, Sweden.

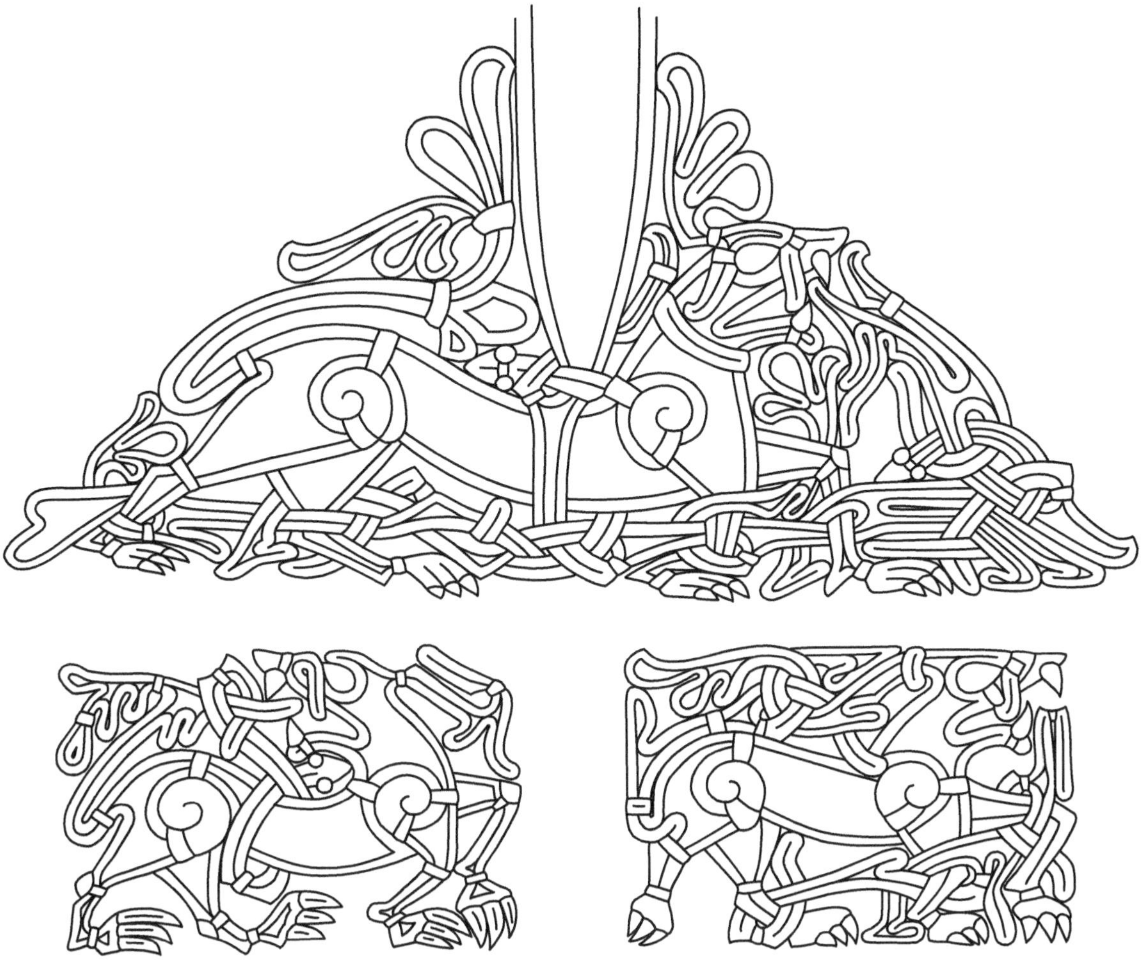

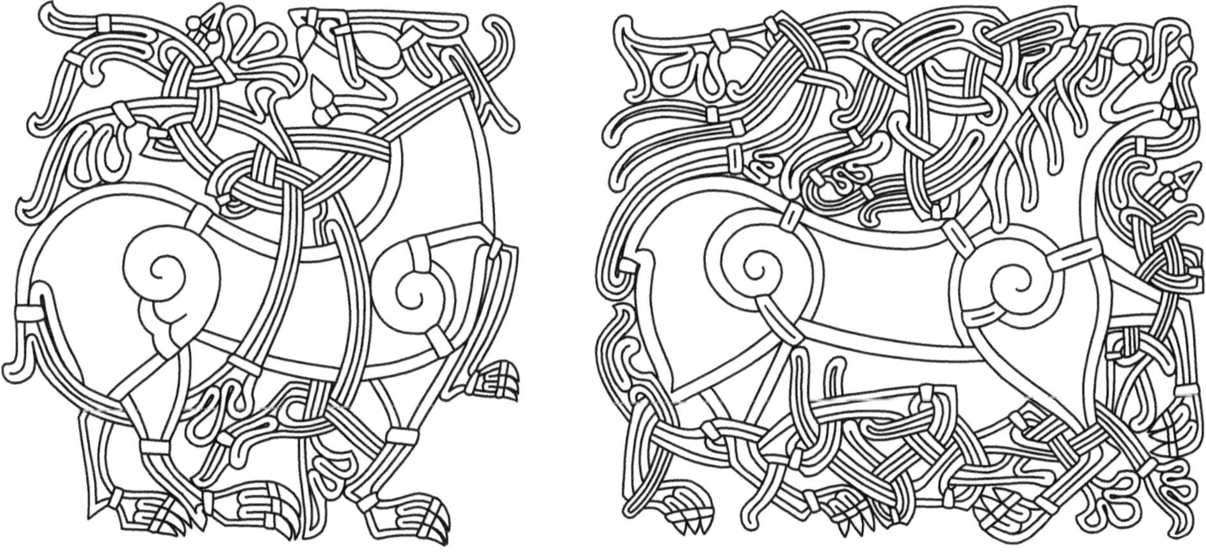

The Bamberg shrine, Bavaria, Germany.

The Cammin shrine, Mecklenburg-Vorpommern, Germany.

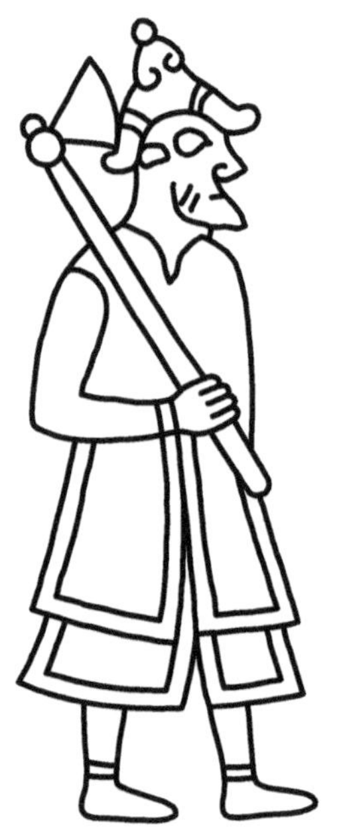

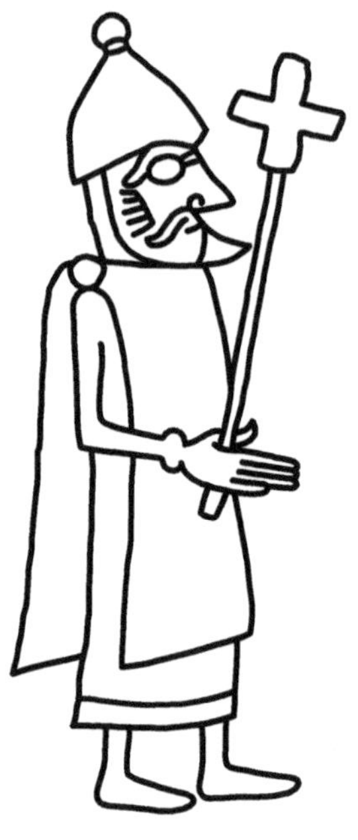

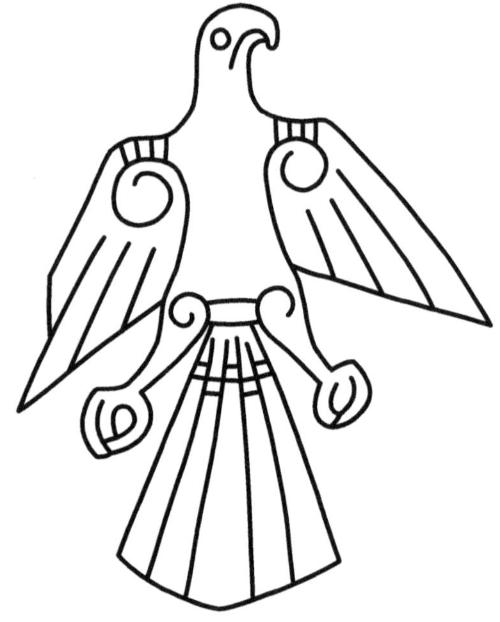

DR 282, Hunnestad, Skåne, Sweden.

DR 290, Sövestad, Skåne, Sweden.

U 692, Väppeby, Uppland, Sweden (Early Urnes Style).

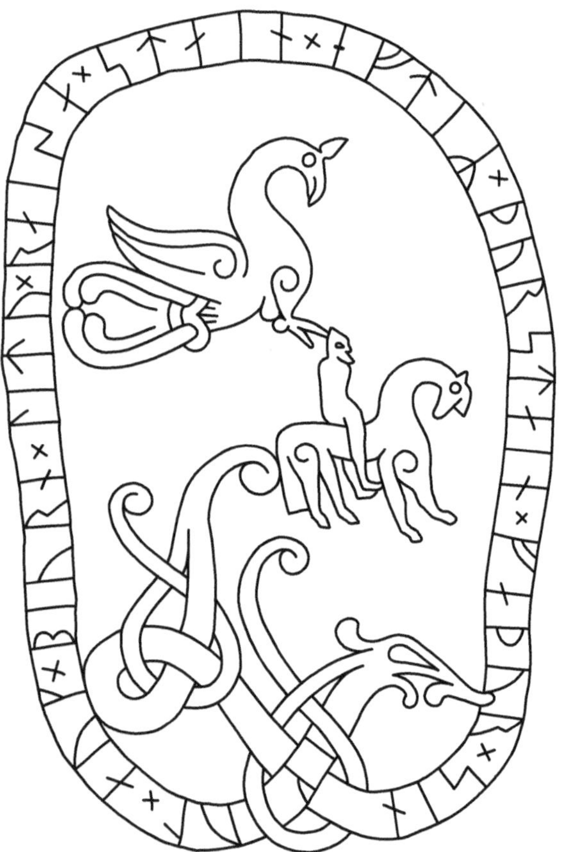

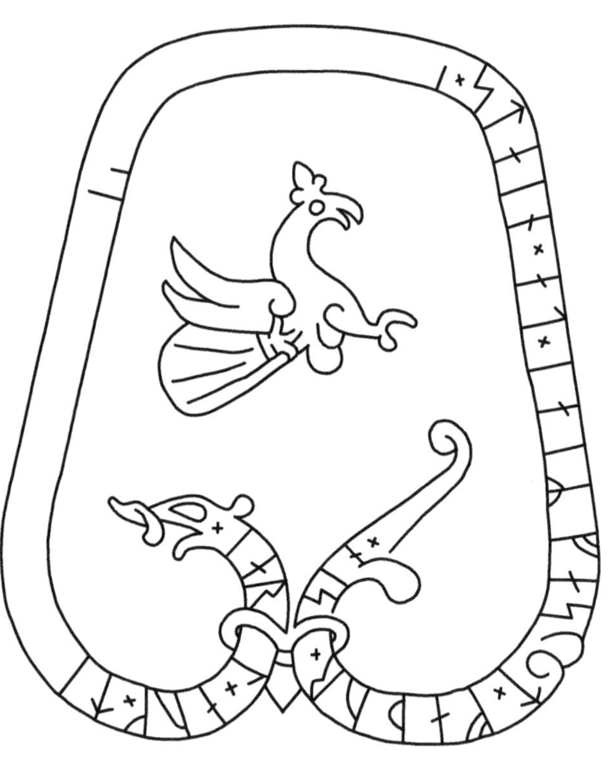

U 448, Harg, Uppland, Sweden (Early Urnes Style).

U 874, Hagby, Uppland, Sweden (Early Urnes Style).